First Ladies of Michigan

First Ladies of Michigan

Revised, Second Edition

Willah Weddon

NOG Press
325B North Clippert Street
Lansing, Michigan 48912

Published 1977
Revised second edition published 1994
Printed in the United States of America

Published by NOG Press
325 B N. Clippert Street Lansing, Michigan 48912

ISBN 0-9638376-0-5

Publisher's Cataloguing in Publication Data
Weddon, Willah
FIRST LADIES OF MICHIGAN
Revised, second edition
Governor's wives * Michigan * Biography
F565 b.W4 9777.4/00992 a B
Library of Congress Card Number: 93-61081

About the Author

During the ten years Willah Weddon was operating her Women's News Bureau at the Capitol in Lansing, she wrote about Michigan's First Ladies.

In the spring of 1977, Dr. Samuel R. Solomon, Professor of Political Science at Eastern Michigan University, brought it to Helen Milliken's attention that there was no written record of the Governor's wives in Michigan. Mrs. Milliken relayed his remarks to Mrs. Weddon.

Combining her experience as a journalist and political writer with her interest in history and research, Weddon set to work. Her book, *First Ladies of Michigan*, was published in the fall of 1977. But there was much more hidden away about the first ladies and Weddon continued collecting information through the years for this new book.

Weddon is a Michigan native with a B.A. degree from Western Michigan University and graduate credits from the University of Michigan. She did some writing for the *Kalamazoo Gazette* while in high school, wrote for the college newspaper, published the *Comstock Coronet* and was Willow Run editor for the *Ypsilanti Press*. She was a correspondent for the *Jackson Citizen Patriot, Lansing State Journal,* and *Detroit Free Press* before establishing the Women's News Bureau at the Capitol.

She is a past president of the Michigan Press Women, a past secretary of the National Federation of Press Women, Inc., and a past president of the Michigan State Medical Auxiliary.

When named the 1972 Woman of Achievement by Michigan Press Women, Weddon was honored by a joint resolution of the Michigan Legislature. She has been awarded more than 80 first place state awards and 13 national awards for writing, photography, public relations, and editing.

Following are the abbreviations, full names and affiliations of organizations that provided pictures for this book:

STATE ARCHIVES   Michigan State Archives of the Bureau of History,
Michigan Department of State

BENTLEY   Michigan Historical Collections at the University of Michigan
Bentley Historical Library

BURTON   Burton Historical Collection, Detroit Public Library

DETROIT NEWS   Reprinted with permission of *The Detroit News*, a Gannett
newspaper, copyright 1993.

Front and back cover photos courtesy of the Michigan Travel Bureau.
Others are credited under the photographs they provided.

To Ed and our Family:
Todd, Carol, and Lisa
Bradley, Kim, Sarah, and Seth
Patrice, Jim, Tyler, and Kelsey
Alex, Colleen, Dane, Randi, Mallory, and Alaina
Amy, Terry, Kimberlee, and Bryan.

Table of Contents

MICHIGAN'S WOMEN LIEUTENANT GOVERNORS

GOVERNOR'S OFFICIAL FAMILY RESIDENCES

❖ Foreword ❖

Those who have held or now hold public office often talk about how important team work is to their success. From the beginning of this nation, Presidents have enjoyed the counsel of their Presidential Cabinet, for instance. Even local office holders need the counsel of others to fulfill their duties. Indeed, there is ample historical evidence of cases where counselors have been very strong positive or, at times unfortunately, negative influences on those who relied on their advice and direction.

The most effective advisers, of course, are those who have the closest relationship with the decision makers, where there is a strong element of mutual trust and loyalty. Willah Weddon reminds us in this fine book, *First Ladies of Michigan*, that the elected leaders of Michigan have benefited profoundly from their spouses' partnership, as have the state's citizens, for that matter. Furthermore, given that Michigan's Governors have been men... a situation, we should hope, which will not be the state's hallmark forever... their counselors and partners have been women.

And a remarkable collection of women it has been, to be sure. From a historical perspective, Michigan has been generally well blessed with good, honest and dedicated governors. After reading *First Ladies of Michigan*, one cannot help but conclude that they were better people in those posts because of the assistance they received from their wives. That is all in hindsight, too, for sadly many of the first ladies were relatively unknown in their own times, and until Willah Weddon dedicated herself to finding more about them, they had been, by and large, relegated to the far corners of our collective history.

As any good historian does, Willah Weddon has placed the sharp light of solid research and writing on the lives of Michigan's First Ladies, and the stories she recounts here are informative, entertaining, and enlightening. She has traveled down this research path previously in her first edition of *First Ladies of Michigan;* but this is more than a simple second edition. It is a much fuller monograph, better because of more extensive research on the author's part along with input from readers of that first book and fellow historians who offered her additional observations and important leads that uncovered heretofore unknown facts about Michigan's First Ladies. The final product is a fine book for the reader, an excellent reference for researchers, and a fitting tribute to the women who contributed so much to Michigan, its governorship, and its history. ❖

Thomas L. Jones, Executive Director
Historical Society of Michigan

❖ Preface ❖

ach First Lady has marched to her own drummer. Some loved the parade and a few would have preferred to lead it. Several couldn't stand the music and opted to drop out. The majority of them, however, kept in step with their governor-husbands. They all contributed, in their own way, something to the history of Michigan.

During the years I worked on researching and re-writing *First Ladies of Michigan,* it became apparent to me that each of these women possessed an admirable strength of character.

Michigan's First Ladies have ranged from pioneers arriving from the East, to farm women and homemakers, to sophisticated society women, and to independent career women.

How much influence social pressure, or lack of it, has had on the women is arguable. For years their chief duties were to raise their children and be good hostesses. As women's roles expanded, so did their responsibilities.

Times have changed since 1842 when Mary Barry kept house and hand-sewed her husband's shirts. Today, Michelle Engler travels around the state filling a public role and continues her law career on a part-time basis. She obviously has more options, but there is bound to be a certain amount of stress.

The one common bond shared by First Ladies is that their husbands are governors. First ladies are not elected officials, draw no salaries, and are expected to fulfill certain conventional roles. Many have entertained Presidents and others have welcomed European Nobility into their homes.

Although their personalities differ drastically, the women share a resilience that may develop from being married to men ambitious in politics and government. In the 1800s they had to spend months alone when their husbands were in Washington or weeks alone when they were at the state capital. Some, like Mary Ann Crapo, ran the family farms while their husbands were in Lansing.

Writing this history was discouraging at times because so little had been recorded about the First Ladies, especially in the early years. The only way to track them down was to read the history of each governor. If there was a mention that the governor had a wife, her name was not necessarily included.

There were moments of utter frustration because no one had saved portraits or photographs of these women who are important to the history of our state. Some of the photographs are poor but it was like hitting the jackpot to find them. And, we may never know what five of them looked like.

Other times it was exhilarating to find a diary kept by one of the women, Mary Sleeper, or letters a First Lady had written. The letters were most often found tucked away in her husband's papers which have been preserved in historical libraries or by historical societies.

As the role of women changed, however, First Ladies have been accorded a more prominent place in the media. Clara Brucker had a hand in this. A journalist by training, she left her own paper trail in newspapers and wrote a book using notes and photographs she'd taken.

It is hoped that this book will fill in the blank pages in the history of Michigan concerning the First Ladies. After all, as Helen Milliken points out, they were there when history was being made. ❖

Willah Weddon, December 1993

❖ Elizabeth S. Cass ❖

Wife of

Territorial Governor General Lewis Cass

1813-1831

lizabeth Spencer Cass was married to Brigadier General Lewis Cass, a governor of the Michigan Territory. He was appointed by the President of the United States and served for five terms, more terms than any other territorial governor of Michigan.[1]

Michigan had not been admitted to the union and there was no state governor. Therefore, Elizabeth is not counted as one of the First Ladies of Michigan. But she served at her husband's side for 18 years in the territorial capital at Detroit. She did, in fact, fill the role of a governor's wife for more years than any other woman in the history of the state. For this reason, she is recognized in this book for her contribution to the formation of the state.

Elizabeth Cass Chapter of the DAR

Described as having a calm, sweet face and gentle manners, Elizabeth, nevertheless, displayed a strength of character which she inherited from her forebearers. Her father, Dr. Joseph Spencer, was a surgeon in the Revolutionary War and served as an aide to his father, General Joseph Spencer. Her mother, Deborah Selden, was the daughter of Colonel Samuel Selden, who was also in the Revolutionary War.

Elizabeth was born on September 17, 1786 in Millington, Connecticut, and raised with educational advantages in a refined home. In later life she made it a practice to read two hours a day. She also was an organizing member of the First Presbyterian Church in 1825.[2]

In March of 1806, 19 year-old Elizabeth married 24 year-old Lewis Cass. Cass had been born in Exeter, New Hampshire, where he studied at Phillips Academy. He practiced law in Marietta, Ohio, served in the war of 1812, and became a Brigadier General.[3] He served in the military in 1813, the army in 1814, and was appointed as Major General by President James Madison.[4]

When General Cass was appointed to replace General William Hull as governor of the newly organized Michigan Territory in 1813, he and Elizabeth moved to Detroit from Ohio.

Their new home was the St. Martin's Mansion on the river bank between what is now Cass Street and Third Street, where Cobo Hall stands. Although it was called a mansion, it was actually constructed with logs and weatherboarded up one story to a sharply peaked roof. Built of oak, the mansion was 40 feet long and 24 feet wide. A visitor in 1826 described the house as very beautiful and surrounded by flourishing orchards and gardens.

For 18 years Elizabeth lived in this house and proved her mettle. She bore seven children and raised the five who survived: Eliza, who never married; Mary, who married Captain Augustus Canfield; Matilda, who married Henry Ledyard; Belle, who married Baron Von Linburg; Lewis Cass, Jr., who never married and died in Rome when serving as American Charge d'Affaires.[5]

While she was busy at home, Elizabeth's husband was off surveying huge tracts of land, negotiating treaties with Indian tribes, promoting settlement of the state, and running Michigan Territorial Council affairs. During his explorations, Cass named Elizabeth Lake after his wife. He was also a founder of the Historical Society of Michigan in 1828.

Detroit was considered the Western Frontier at this time and pioneer families were only beginning to push out along trails into the uncharted wilderness.

Detroit home of Lewis and Elizabeth Cass

As was vital to their survival in those days, families arriving too late to travel on to new home sites and build log cabins before freezing weather, would spend winters in already established households. Elizabeth did her share. Some guests stayed for a meal, others for a week, and some for a month or more.[6]

Elizabeth was also expected to entertain every distinguished visitor to Michigan in the Governor's Mansion. She earned a reputation for always being a gracious and hospitable hostess.

Her granddaughter later wrote, "Half-breed servants were not very competent and the burden fell on Mrs. Cass of putting the pork in brine, smoking hams, and supplying the larder with pies, plum cake, preserves, and dried apples. All this personal labor added (was in addition) to the clothing and educating of five children. One wonders how, as my mother has often told me, she always found time to read for two hours every day."

President Andrew Jackson appointed Cass as Secretary of War from 1831 to 1836 and U.S. Minister to France from 1836 to 1842. In 1836 their St. Martin's Mansion was cut in two and removed to other sites. When he returned from France, they had a frame house built on the northwest corner of Fort Street and Cass Avenue.

Cass was elected to the U.S. Senate in 1845 and resigned in 1848 to become Michigan's first candidate for President. He lost the race to Whig candidate, Zachary Taylor. He returned to the Senate in 1848 until 1857, and served as secretary of state from 1857 to 1860 for President James Buchanan.

Elizabeth Cass died on March 31, 1853, 12 years before her husband. He died on June 17, 1866. Both were buried in Elmwood Cemetery of Detroit. The Elizabeth Cass Chapter of the Daughters of the American Revolution installed a commemorative bronze marker on the site of their graves in 1972. ❖

❖ Historical Note

Matilda Cass, daughter of General Lewis and Elizabeth Cass, married Henry Ledyard. They had a son, Henry B., who had a son Henry, whose son Henry Ledyard lives in Grosse Pointe Farms today and has a son, Henry B. Ledyard.

❖ Emily V. Mason ❖

Sister of

Acting Governor Stevens T. Mason

1831 to 1835

The Mason family was an exceptional one and played a significant role in the development of Michigan while a territory and during its first years of statehood.

Stevens T. Mason's great-grandfather, George Mason, was a friend of George Washington and Patrick Henry, and he wrote Virginia's first constitution.[1] His son was Stevens T. Mason, a U.S. Senator, and his son was General John Thomson Mason, a lawyer who was appointed as secretary and acting governor of the Michigan Territory in 1830.

State Archives

When General John Thomson Mason left in 1831 to go to Texas, his son, Stevens Thomson Mason, was appointed as secretary and acting governor by President Andrew Jackson. Except for a short interim, he held this post until he was elected governor in 1835.

Stevens Thomson Mason's mother and sisters (there were six) had entertained for him in their Detroit home.[2] But when he was named acting governor in 1834, it was his sister, Emily Virginia, who served as official mistress of the house.

Twenty year-old Emily and her brother were very close. He was about three years older than she, and the two were often seen out riding together.

No brother ever had a sister more loyal to his ambitions than did "Tom" Mason. She was interested in politics and helped him with his documents, recalling, "I was always saying to Thomson, 'Use fewer words.'"[3]

As his hostess, Emily entertained her brother's guests and some of his growing popularity could be traced to the accomplishments of his talented sister.

Emily had just returned from a season in Washington where she had been delighted with the debates participated in by Webster, Clay, Calhoun, and others, when she recalled: "I came to know the lovely Madame Servier of the French Legation, Sir

Charles Vaughan and Mr. Pakingham of the English Embassy, and Mr. Calderon de la Barca, whose charming wife I found again in Paris and Madrid after many years."[4]

Governor Mason's mother and father returned to Detroit in 1835, the year he was nominated for governor at the Democratic-Republicans of Michigan Convention held there on August 24, 1835. He was elected in October. Michigan was admitted to the Union in 1837 and he was elected to a second term which began on January 2, 1838.

In November of 1838, Mason married Julia Elizabeth Phelps from New York and she assumed the role of First Lady. Emily left then to travel, but returned after the Mason's first child, Stevens IV, was born on August 1, 1839. Mason wrote to another sister, Laura, "You have yet to see your nephew… In a few days he mounts his short dresses… the first great epoch in his onward march to manhood. I shall turn him over to you and Emily when you arrive, and rest assured you'll have your hands full, for he is already the very personification of mischief."[5]

Although Mason retired from office in 1840 and moved to New York, he and Emily corresponded until his death in 1843. Emily never married. She later returned to Virginia where she took an active role in the Civil War for the Confederacy.

It was Emily who talked to Governor Fred Warner when he was in Washington for the 1905 inauguration of Theodore Roosevelt about her wish that the remains of her brother be brought back to Detroit. She wanted him "brought home" from the tomb in New York to the site of his most eminent achievements.[6]

Arrangements were made and 91 year-old Emily was on hand for the reinterment ceremonies honoring Mason in Capitol Park.

"Miss Mason and her little great grandnephew cast flowers upon the casket as it slowly sank out of sight, the former retaining one rose from the bouquet which she held back as a cherished souvenir of a moment which was, probably, the proudest of her life. There followed the parting salute to the dead from the firing party and the bugle call of 'Taps.'"[7]

When a bronze statue of Mason was unveiled in Capitol Park in 1908, Emily was again present for the event. At the close of the ceremonies, the band played "Dixie," in her honor.[8]

Emily died later in New York and was buried there. Mary, the youngest sister, was buried in Elmwood Cemetery of Detroit, along with a nephew of Mason's who had changed his name to Stevens T. Mason.[9] ❖

Stevens T. Mason
State Archives

❖ Historical Note

Edward Mundy, lieutenant governor during 1835 to 1840, served as acting governor of Michigan during fairly frequent absences of Stevens T. Mason following his marriage. Mason completed his term, however, so the situation differs from those lieutenant governors who assumed the office full-time after a governor resigned his position. Mundy's wife was therefore not considered a First Lady of Michigan.

❖ Julia Phelps Mason ❖

Wife of

Governor Stevens T. Mason

1835 through 1839

 lthough Stevens Thomson Mason was called Michigan's "Boy Governor," he was actually a 27 year-old bachelor governor when he married Julia Elizabeth Phelps in New York.

A beautiful girl with dark hair and fine features, Julia was almost seven years his junior at the time of their unostentatious wedding on November 1, 1838. She was the daughter of a moderately wealthy New York leather merchant, Thaddeus Phelps.

Mason was negotiating a $5 million loan for Michigan when he first met Julia while a guest in her father's house. The loan caused him considerable difficulty later in his political career although he had been authorized to borrow the money by the state legislature.

"In sweetness of character and real worth, she surpasses every other woman I have ever known," Mason wrote to his sister, Emily, in Detroit. Emily had served as hostess for Mason and she was credited with helping him rise from a territorial secretary at age 19, to acting governor of the Michigan Territory, at age 22, and on to be the first elected governor of Michigan at age 24 and re-elected at age 26.

Bentley

Julia and Mason remained in New York three weeks after their wedding and then made the long trip back to Detroit. Their marriage came as a great surprise to the people out-state, but in Detroit it was quickly hailed as a major social event.

Julia was considered a very fine hostess, but she didn't seem to be able to handle the frontier, as she regarded her new home. She had good reason to believe Michigan was wild, compared to New York State, because the political situation had grown volatile. There were threats on Mason's life and she feared for him.[1]

In less than six months, Julia packed up and left for New York with Mason. He returned without her. In July he made the two week trip back to New York, sending word to Detroit in August that Julia had given birth to a son, Stevens T. Mason IV. The boy died before he was 5 years of age.

A short time later Mason arrived to tend to his duties in Michigan, but returned to his wife and child in early autumn. His mother went with him back to New York and died there in November. He was to leave office as governor on the first of January (1840) and he said he did so "without one sigh of regret."[2]

The couple was living in New York when their two other children were born: Dorthea Eliza, in October 1840; and Thaddeus Phelps, on March 11, 1842. Mason, meanwhile, made one final trip to Michigan to sell his household goods and left Detroit forever.

Building a new law practice was difficult, but Julia remained "loyal and serene" at his side. On January 3, 1843, however, after a three day illness, Mason died at the age of 31. Newspapers of the day reported the cause as suppressed scarlet fever. Sending word to Detroit, his father wrote, "Julia is in a state of distraction." Mason's body was placed in the vault of his father-in-law and he was buried in the Phelps family plot in Marble Cemetery of New York City.[3]

According to the Phelps family genealogy, their son, Thaddeus, died when he was 3 years old, two years after Mason's death; and the widowed Julia married William Henry McVickar before her death in 1870. The Mason's only surviving child, Dorthea, married Colonel Edward Wright of Newark, New Jersey. Dorthea had two sons; Captain William Wright and Edward H. Wright, Jr. ❖

Stevens T. Mason
State Archives

❖ **Historical Note**

By a 1905 act of the state legislature, Governor Fred Warner appointed a three man commission to go to New York and bring the remains of Stevens T. Mason back to Michigan. The body was reinterred under the foundations of the old Capitol Building where Mason had presided as the first governor of the new state of Michigan. The building had burned down in 1893 and the following year the site in downtown Detroit had become Capitol Park. Mason's only surviving child, Dorthea Mason Wright, and his sister, Emily, attended the reinterment ceremonies.

Three years later, 1908, a life-size statue of Mason was placed on the site where he was buried. It was made from the bronze of old cannon donated by the War Department.

In 1955, during renovation of the park, the casket was taken up and there was a move to have it brought to Lansing. While this was being debated, the body was held in the Wayne County Morgue. Detroit won the argument and Mason's ashes were placed under his statue in Capitol Park.[4]

Courtesy of David M. Edgar

❖ Juliana T. Woodbridge ❖

Wife of

Governor William Woodbridge

1840 and 1841

The wedding of 20 year-old Juliana Trumbull and William Woodbridge in Hartford, Connecticut, on June 9, 1806, was a dignified social event.

Juliana was the beautiful daughter of noted jurist and poet, Judge John Trumbull and his wife, Sarah Hubbard of Hartford. Born April 23, 1786, Juliana was a descendant of William the Conqueror. She had attended the Litchfield Academy, where Woodbridge had spent a year preparing for his Connecticut bar examination.

It has been written that Juliana was a natural poet and wrote quite a large number of verses, some of which were preserved in a printed memorial at the time of her death.[1] Other sources, however, attribute the poetry to a cousin of Woodbridge, Sarah Backus.

Born on August 20, 1780, in Norwich, Connecticut, Woodbridge had followed his parents to Marietta, Ohio, in late 1791. He returned East after about five years to continue his education and by 1804 he was licensed to practice law both in Connecticut and Ohio. After he returned to Ohio, he and Juliana corresponded for two years. He then traveled back east for their wedding.

Juliana, six years younger than Woodbridge, set up housekeeping in Marietta in the house he had built before their wedding. It was a very large, two-story house with two huge trees and a wooden fence in front. During the next eight years he built up a fairly successful law practice and they lived in comfortable circumstances. Their home was convenient... and moderately elegant.[2]

Lewis Cass, now governor of the Michigan Territory, had been a close friend of Woodbridge when they were young in Marietta. When Cass offered the office of Michigan Territorial Secretary to Woodbridge, he felt prospects were better in Detroit and accepted. On January 1, 1815, he took the oath of office and began a two week journey to Detroit.

Juliana did not accompany him as she was expecting their first child, Juliana Trumbull, who was born on September 12, 1815. After the baby arrived, she was concerned about traveling with the infant on the long trip through the "Black Swamp," and didn't leave for Detroit until early 1816.

Five more children were born to the couple: William Leverett was born on July 2, 1817; John, on May 2, 1820; Lucy Maria, July 22, 1822; Henrietta Sarah, on January 25, 1824; Dudley Backus, on February 19, 1826. John died at the age of 4 months and Henrietta died when she was 5 years old.

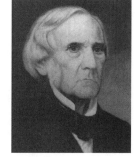

William Woodbridge
State Archives

In September of 1819, Woodbridge was elected as the first delegate to Congress from the Michigan Territory and left on the three month trip to Washington. Juliana, expecting their third child, stayed home with the family. John was born in May by caesarean section, and fortunately Woodbridge was back in Michigan in June. The baby boy died in September.

About that time, for some unknown reason, the women in Detroit ostracized Juliana and one of them was Mary Sophia Spencer, Cass' sister. Until the situation was remedied, Woodbridge withdrew his family from the social life of the city. This conflict also caused an almost total breach in the friendship between Woodbridge and Cass.[3]

When he first came to Michigan, Woodbridge had bought a large French strip farm and house in Spring Wells Township, near Detroit. Later he bought an adjoining farm and by the late 1820s the homestead was established with 1,000 foot frontage on the Detroit River and a depth inland of more than three miles.

They developed the land and in 1838 planted 2,000 fruit trees, forming two large orchards with more than 20 varieties of apples. Speckle Pears were planted in another orchard and became a Woodbridge Farm specialty. They shipped produce by the barrel to Boston, New York, Philadelphia, and Baltimore.[4]

In 1839, they built a new two-story stone house with a view of the Detroit River. They also had a stable, icehouse, and a barn on the property.

Meanwhile, Woodbridge served as acting governor of the Michigan Territory four times while his neighbor, General Lewis Cass, was absent from the office. But when statehood was gained, Woodbridge was the second governor to be elected and was the only Whig governor ever elected in Michigan. He served little more than a year, from January 7, 1840, to February 3, 1841, when he was elected by the state legislature to serve as a U.S. Senator. (Until 1913, U.S. Senators were elected by their state legislatures, rather than by popular vote).

Juliana was a refined, retiring woman and did not get involved in political affairs; although, Woodbridge kept her well apprised of happenings in Washington through his letters. She entertained a great deal and they welcomed guests in the most beautiful room in their home, the Governor's Library. Early historians included Juliana when they wrote about Woodbridge by saying, "Side by side with her husband, with the highest type of domestic and social graces, she manifested a keen intellectuality."[5]

After completing his six-year term in the Senate, Woodbridge retired from public life and the couple continued to live on the farm they loved so much. It became a constant legal battle, however, to preserve their land from high taxes and from being absorbed and sub-divided by the growing city of Detroit.

There were many appeals to the courts and delays led by 77 year-old Woodbridge. In one appeal, he told the court that it was threatening the security of a beautiful, law-abiding woman by removing her from her residence of 40 years. The courts, he maintained, were denying her a final wish… to die at home. Through his constant efforts, the couple was able to live out their days on their farm estate in Spring Wells.

In 1854 their eldest daughter, Juliana Backus, and her two children came to live with her parents. She had married her father's first cousin, Henry Backus.

Juliana died at the age of 74 on February 19, 1860, after years of being an invalid, and was buried in the private farmland burial ground. Within a year it was closed and the bodies moved to Detroit's

Home of Governor William and Juliana Woodbridge, which was torn down in 1873. It was located on Woodbridge Street.

Elmwood Cemetery. They were survived by three of their children… Juliana, William Leverett, Dudley… and seven grandchildren.

Woodbridge continued to live on the farm until his death on October 20, 1861. He was also buried in Elmwood Cemetery. Portions of the farm were soon sold to city dwellers. Today the green acres of the spring-fed, sandy soil are covered by buildings and the asphalt roads of inner-Detroit. ❖

❖ **Historical Note**

Following Governor Woodbridge's resignation from office on March 4, 1841, Lieutenant Governor James W. Gordon became acting governor.

❖ Mary Hudun Gordon ❖

Wife of

Governor James Wright Gordon

1841

 ary Hudun was from Geneva, New York, and it is assumed that she met James Gordon when he was studying law and teaching at Geneva College.

Mary and Gordon came to Michigan during the 1835 land rush. They settled in Marshall and he became a prominent attorney in the young town. They had five children: Anna, Catharine, Mary G., Edwin, and Alfred.[1]

Unfortunately, very little information has been preserved about Mary. She apparently kept a fine home and devoted her time to their children. Their eldest son was later reported to be studying law in Chicago.

Gordon was elected to the state senate in 1839 and lead a campaign to make Marshall the capital of Michigan when it was moved from Detroit. He was so confident of the outcome that he built a beautiful Greek Revival house that same year, hoping that it would serve as the Governor's Mansion. The future Executive Mansion was built at the top of Capitol Hill, as it is still called, overlooking the site where the Capitol Building was expected to stand.

Obviously ambitious for his own career, Gordon had an "understanding" with some powerful authorities that Ann Arbor was to be given the university, Jackson the penitentiary, and Marshall the capital… all along the road running from Detroit to Chicago.[2]

When the final vote was taken by the Michigan Legislature in 1847, however, Lansing was chosen to be the site of the state capital. This dashed the hopes of the town of Marshall and was a setback to Gordon's political plans. But Mary and their family continued to live in the mansion.

It is ironical that there was a Governor's Mansion in the state eight years before the Capitol Building in Lansing was erected. But an actual residence was not provided for governors and their families until 1969, more than 100 years later.

Gordon was elected lieutenant governor in 1840 and became acting governor when Governor William Woodbridge resigned to go to the U.S. Senate, on February 23, 1841. Gordon served in this capacity for ten months and a week. Later, President Zachary Taylor appointed him to the consular service in South America and he died there in December of 1853 under mysterious circumstances.

Mary was with Gordon in Brazil when he died and returned to New York. It was reported that he had bronchial trouble and, in a coughing fit, fell to his death from a second story balcony. His obituary did not appear in the Marshall newspaper until the following February.[3]

Mary retained possession of the Governor's Mansion after her husband's death, but used it later as rental property until she sold it in 1882. In 1966, the house was given to the Mary Marshall Chapter of the Daughters of the American Revolution. It has been restored by the DAR and serves as a meeting place and museum. It is on the Michigan Historical Register and the National Register of Historic Places. ❖

This Early Greek Revival home was intended to be Michigan's first Governor's Mansion in 1839. Now it is owned by the Mary Marshall Chapter, DAR.   Courtesy of John J. Collins

❖ Mary K. Barry ❖

Wife of

Governor John S. Barry

1842 through 1845 also 1850 and 1851

ither Mary Barry was the brunt of cruel political gossip, an overly sensitive woman, or an eccentric. Stories related by her peers in their later years concerning her activities are singular at best.

Mary Kidder was born on August 25, 1801, in Grafton, Vermont. With her New England accent, she called her husband, "Mister Bahrrie," from the time of their marriage in 1824. His nickname for her was "Polly."[1]

After their marriage, John Steward Barry was in charge of an academy in Atlanta, Georgia, for two years and he studied law during that time. The couple moved to Michigan in 1831, living first in White Pigeon and three years later moving to Constantine. He became a successful businessman with a warehouse and fleet of grain and flour boats operating on the St. Joseph River. He was also active in politics. He served as senator and later, governor for three terms.[2]

Mary was described as tall, angular, cross-eyed, and in marked contrast to the rotundity of Governor Barry. She was apparently a sensitive woman and, if she heard remarks made by those in her community, had reason to be.

Courtesy of Dr. Marvin Vercler

In a sketch by Emily Comstock, given before the Abiel Fellows Chapter of the Daughters of the American Revolution and filed with the historical records at the Three Rivers Library, memories of Mary Barry by many older men and women of Constantine were reported. One description said she "brewed and stewed and boiled and baked and washed and ironed and when not hard at work in the duties of the kitchen, she busied her ever active fingers in making ruffled shirts for the Governor out of the finest linen.

"She did all this even though there were always two, sometimes three, and even four, strong capable maids in the house."[3] It was also noted that anyone wanting to see Mary Barry need not expect to meet her at a social event but should go to her house where they'd be ushered to her in the kitchen.

She was a "curiosity," according to one man, because she was so seldom seen in community social affairs. Others said she had certain strong characteristics that were peculiarly hers. One of these was her frugality.

Mary was given credit, however, for her charitable acts. She was known to hunt for herbs and plants in the woods and use them to brew medicine to carry to the sick. One of those who knew her intimately, told the following story:

"At one time there was living in the Barry household a young man who later enlisted for Civil War service. Many and many a time this young man was asked to take a basket, one of the proverbially well filled kind, to someone who was ill, someone who was unfortunate, or someone who would especially appreciate the delicacies it held. And always there was this admonition: 'Don't say anything about this, Charles.'"[4]

Actually, Charles Dudley was their adopted son.[5] The Barrys had no children of their own and were very fond of him. In his will, Barry left half his fortune to his brother, Charles H. Barry, and divided the other half equally among Charles and the three children of Aldis Barry, his deceased brother.

The state capital was in Detroit during Barry's first two terms as governor. Several people from Constantine rode on a hay wagon to Detroit for Barry's inauguration. They kept warm by sitting on planks placed over sealed crocks of hot water.[6]

When he was elected for his third term, four years later, the capital had been moved to Lansing. Mary went with him to Lansing on at least one occasion, but obviously wasn't comfortable there. During that visit, she left the festivities given in her honor to return home. She had to get home at once so the grease she had been saving to convert into soap wouldn't spoil.[7]

The fact that Mary preferred staying in Constantine may be the real reason Governor Barry refused to live in a house which was reportedly built in 1849 to serve as the Governor's Mansion in Lansing. He declared the house was too small for the Executive Mansion, according to an unidentified historian in a report in the *Lansing State Journal,* nearly a century later. It became the home of a lieutenant governor, and other state officials lived there in subsequent years until it was deeded to Orlando Mack Barnes, a railroad pioneer in the state.

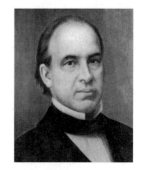

John S. Barry
State Archives

Considering his reputation for thriftiness, it seems unlikely that size was the real reason for Barry's refusal. The house was constructed at the corner of Allegan Street and Capitol Avenue, and still contained some of the original pioneer logs when it was moved in 1925 to another site.

Society may have frowned on Mary, but in her own way she must have filled Governor Barry's needs as he was regarded as an exceptionally good governor. When he retired from public life, he devoted his remaining years to operating his large store in Constantine.

The couple had built a large Greek Revival house in 1836. But after the Governor had served two terms in office they had another, larger one erected in 1847. They sold their smaller house and moved into their new home in 1849, before he began serving his third term. Another reason for not wanting to move to Lansing.

Mary died on March 30, 1869, and Barry died less than a year later, on January 14, 1870. They were both buried in Constantine. ❖

Governor John and Mary Barry lived in this house, 280 North Washington Street in Constantine, until they built a larger one. It is now the Governor John S. Barry Museum and is maintained by the Governor Barry Historical Society.   State Archives

❖ Historical Note

The house the Barrys built and lived in until 1849 has been maintained as a museum by the Governor Barry Historical Society and Constantine Community Center since 1945. It is listed on the National Register of Historic Homes and is located at 260 North Washington Street in Constantine. It is open to the public on holidays and by appointment.

❖ Lucretia L. Felch ❖

Wife of

Governor Alpheus Felch

1846 and 1847

ucretia Williams Lawrence was the eldest of nine children in the family of Judge Wolcott Lawrence, who was the first lawyer to settle in Monroe. Born on December 31, 1817, she was said to be the first white child born in the French settlement of Monroe.[1]

Lucretia met Alpheus Felch when he stopped in Monroe for a few days to meet her father while making a journey to the South in 1833. A native of Limerick, Maine, born on September 28, 1804, he had been practicing law in Maine for three years, until he was advised to go south for his health.

Despite an invitation to remain in Monroe, Felch continued as far as Cincinnati, Ohio, where he became ill with cholera. After recovering, he decided it would be wise to wait for cooler weather before traveling on and returned to the settlement.[2] He soon gave up all thoughts of leaving the area and Lucretia undoubtedly influenced this decision.

His letters to her in 1836 began with "Dear Lucretia" until they were married on September 14, 1837. From that time on they began with "My Dear Wife."[3] They lived in Monroe for about six years until they moved to Ann Arbor and made it their permanent home.

Stewards of the State/Detroit News

A small but forceful woman, Lucretia had been raised in a politically oriented family. Her father had served as a member of the first and second sessions of the Second and Third Annual Territorial Legislatures in Detroit, 1826 through 1829, and was delegate to the First Convention of Assent in Ann Arbor during September of 1836.[4]

Lucretia's focus, however, was on caring for Felch and their eight children. Caroline was born on October 22, 1838; Elizabeth H., on March 20, 1841; Emma Lucretia, on March 21, 1843; Arthur Willis, in 1845; and Theodore Alpheus, on March 30, 1847, just 26 days after his father resigned his gubernatorial position and became a U.S. Senator.[5]

Three more children were born to the couple: Florence Cornelia, on January 9, 1852; Francis Lawrence, on January 3, 1854; and Helen Louise, on February 6, 1858. Florence died when she was 10 years old and Emma died at age 31.

Feltch was elected governor of Michigan after serving in the state legislature, 1835 to 1837; as state bank commissioner, 1838 to 1839; Auditor General, 1842; and on the Michigan Supreme Court, 1842 to 1845. He resigned, however, in March of 1847 when he was elected to the U.S. Senate for a full six year term. At the close of this term in 1853, he was appointed president of a commission to settle Spanish and Mexican land claims in California, by President Franklin Pierce.

After three years in California, the family returned to Michigan because they felt educational facilities were better here for their children. Back in Ann Arbor, Felch practiced law and later became a law professor at the University of Michigan.[6] He was also president of the Michigan Pioneer and Historical Society.

In later years, one of her sons wrote his recollections of Lucretia: "Mother was about the average height for a woman and looked as if she were quite frail. She probably never weighed over a hundred pounds. But she was a very active and forceful individual. Her eyes were large and blue in color, her hair light brown, her nose very thin and quite prominent.

"Because his (Father's) duties required him to be absent from home for days or weeks at a time, his wife found her responsibilities burdensome. She complained bitterly of this condition of affairs but she stuck to her work...

"While we always lived, as I remember, in a very large house, I never knew of her doing much of the household work. She always had two robust German maids to do that. Of course, Father's high position in public life required her to do much entertaining and thrust upon her many social duties. But she was thoroughly capable as a hostess and met all such affairs in a most hospitable and gracious manner.

"She was of a modest and retiring disposition, and her heart was in the care of her house and her children. She had a fine education and was always a constant and intelligent reader. In her letters to Father, she often asks him to bring her books

on history, or biography, or the better novels, from the public library.

"She was a very religious woman, very active in all church work and a strict follower of the Presbyterian faith. Her house was the haven of innumerable preachers, delegates to conventions, etc. A most charitable and sympathetic woman. She did allow the girls to have all the social diversions they wished, but we boys were not allowed to go to dancing school."[7]

Alpheus Felch
State Archives

22

Concerned about her husband's health, Lucretia wrote to her daughter, Libbie, in March of 1881, "Your father is feeling very tired and glad the term is so near over. He had thought perhaps he would resign his position at the end of the year, but I think the proffessors (sic) will persuade him not to."[8] She did not mention her health, but she died the next year in Ann Arbor on July 30, 1882, and was buried in Forest Hill Cemetery of Ann Arbor.

Felch lived 14 years after Lucretia's death and was living with their daughter, Elizabeth (Mrs. E. H. Cole), in Ann Arbor when he died at age 91 on June 13, 1896. He was survived by five of their children, 16 grandchildren and two great-grandchildren.

The couple's eldest daughter, Caroline, married Claudius B. Grant of Lansing, who also served in state government. He was a University of Michigan Regent, a Speaker of the House of Representatives, and a Michigan Supreme Court Justice from 1890 to 1909. He wrote, *Governors of the Territory and State of Michigan, Bulletin No. 16,* which was published by the Michigan Historical Commission of Lansing in 1928.[9] ❖

Lucretia Felch's childhood home in Monroe was thought to have been built about 1825 by her father, Judge Walcott Lawrence. It was razed in 1946.   Bentley

❖ Historical Note

When Governor Felch resigned on March 4, 1847, Lieutenant Governor William Greenly of Adrian filled out the remainder of the term as acting governor.

❖ Elizabeth W. Hubbard Greenly ❖

Wife of

Acting Governor William L. Greenly

1847

E lizabeth W. Hubbard Greenly was from Massachusetts and was the wife of William Greenly while he was serving ten months as acting governor of Michigan. She was the second of his three wives.

William L. Greenly was born on September 18, 1813, in Hamilton, New York, where he was raised and studied law for three years. He was admitted to the bar in 1833 and began to practice in Eaton, New York. A year later in December of 1834, he married Sarah A. Dascomb from Hamilton.[1]

Sarah apparently died and Greenly moved to Adrian in 1836 to set up another law practice. After an unsuccessful bid to fill a vacancy in the state legislature in 1837, he ran again and was elected to the senate for a two-year term in 1839 and returned to office in 1842-1843.[2]

After being elected to the Michigan Senate, Greenly made a trip East where he and his second wife, 22 year-old Elizabeth Hubbard, were married on June 11, 1840, in Northampton, Massachusetts. The couple had two sons; Marshall H. and William M. The latter was born about the time Greenly was elected lieutenant governor in 1845.[3]

When Alpheus Felch resigned to take a seat in the U.S. Senate on March 3, 1847, Greenly became acting governor and served to the end of the term. He returned to their home in Adrian and was elected justice of the peace, holding the office for 12 years.

The Greenlys had two homes in Adrian and one of them was located at the foot of what is now Greenly Street, according to Charles Lindquist, Curator of the Lenawee County Historical Museum.

Elizabeth died in September 1857, at the age of 39, leaving Greenly with two teen-age sons. During 1858 Greenly served as mayor of Adrian, and a year later, October 25, 1859, he married a local woman, Maria Hart. Cemetery records show a Baby Sarah E. died at the age of two months and another Sarah E. died in April of 1862. It is quite possible these little girls were named for Greenly's first wife. At the time it was a fairly common practice to name a baby for one that had deceased and not unusual to name a child after a wife who had died. If the middle initial represented Elizabeth, the infants may have been named for both of his previous wives.

Greenly lived until November 29, and was buried on December 2, 1883. He was survived by Maria and one son, Marshall, who was a conductor on the Lake Shore Railroad and resided in Elkhart, Indiana. His other son, William H., had died at the age of 23.[4]

Maria lived until April 10, 1897, and Marshall until June 16, 1898. All the Greenlys, except Sarah Dascomb are buried in the family plot, Oakwood Cemetery of Adrian. ❖

❖ Almira Cadwell Ransom ❖

Wife of

Governor Epaphroditus Ransom

1848 and 1849

Both Almira and Epaphroditus Ransom came from distinguished families in New England. They moved to Michigan because several members of his family had come to the Kalamazoo area and sent back glowing reports about the beauty and advantages of the new location.

Almira Cadwell Ransom was the daughter of Wyllys J. Cadwell, a representative citizen and a successful merchant of Montpelier, Vermont. He was among the first settlers of the new capital after its removal from Vergennes which had been the seat of government since the admission of the state into the Union.[1]

According to the Kalamazoo County census, Almira was 44 years old in 1850. Her tombstone is imprinted with the date of her death being March 17, 1877, at the age of 73. Her obituary in the *Kalamazoo Daily Telegraph* states she was 72 when she died. All this information leads to the conclusion she was born sometime between 1804 and 1806.[2]

Epaphroditus' father, Ezekiel Ransom, enlisted in the Revolutionary War when he was only 14 years old and served under Officer Samuel Fletcher. He continued enlisting until the close of the war. For a time he was on the non-commissioned staff of General George Washington. At the close of the war Ezekiel married General Samuel and Mehitable Fletcher's daughter, Lucinda. The couple had 12 children and Epaphroditus was their eldest son and fourth child, born on March 24, 1798.[3]

Ransom graduated from law school in Northampton, Massachusetts, and opened a law practice in his hometown of Townshend, Vermont. He soon entered local politics, was elected justice of the peace for the county, served five years (1825 to 1830 inclusive) and was re-elected in 1833.

"He was a Jeffersonian Democrat politically, which was about equal to the unpardonable sin in old Federal Vermont, but for all that the constituency elected him as their representative to the legislature from Townshend township for the years 1826 and 1827."[4]

The assembly convened at Montpelier and it was here that Almira met Ransom. They were married on February 21, 1827, and returned immediately to their new home in

Epaphroditus Ransom
State Archives

Townshend. During the next seven years he practiced law and three of their children were born. Wyllys Cadwell, named for Almira's father, was born April 28, 1828. Elizabeth W. was born September 22, 1830, and died shortly after her first birthday (October 5, 1831). Antoinette E. was born a year later on October 11, 1832.

By 1834, Ransom's brother and a sister, with their families, and an unmarried brother had moved to Michigan. He and Almira decided to join them. He closed his business, they loaded their belongings on wagons and headed west with their two young children. It took them a month by wagon, canal, steamboat, and wagon again, to arrive in Bronson on November 14, 1834.

The small village of about 20 houses and 100 people was called Bronson at that time, after Titus Bronson who had originally taken up the land. He sold his interests to new proprietors who changed the name of the place to Kalamazoo which was the Indian name.

Since old Titus was moving, Almira and Epaphroditus took over his log house. It could not have been an easy winter for Almira with a 2 year-old and a 6 year-old cooped up in a log cabin "with snow and sleet drifting through the roof and the long-drawn howl of the famished wolf resounding frequently beneath their windows."[5]

Ransom had immediately begun his law practice in the community and by the next fall had built an office with a house next door for the family. They lived here about six years. During this time there were several important events in their lives. In 1837, Michigan was admitted to the Federal Union and Governor Stevens T. Mason appointed Ransom as the first circuit court judge in western Michigan and an associate justice of the Supreme Court.[6]

This required a great deal of travel, usually by horseback, and he had long distances to cover. Another son, Eugene Beauharnais, was born to the couple on March 31, 1837, and died in August of 1837 or 1838. Records vary on the date. Almira must have spent many days and weeks alone with their young children and a sickly baby.

The Ransoms had their house moved in 1841 to a large farm site which became well known for its sheep and cattle and productive orchards. Ransom was also a founder of the village of Augusta, 12 miles east of Kalamazoo, during this period.

In 1843, Governor John S. Barry appointed him as chief justice of the Michigan Supreme Court. Four years later, in 1847, Ransom lost the nomination for U.S. Senator, but was nominated for governor by the Democratic party.

During that same year, the Ransoms built a beautiful Greek Revival style home in what is now downtown Kalamazoo. "It was an establishment for a gentleman of that period," according to the *Kalamazoo Gazette*. Ransom won the election and resigned from the high court to take office as governor in 1848. He was the first governor to be inaugurated in Lansing as the capital had previously been in Detroit. The ceremony was held in a two-story frame building known as the State House.

After completing his term as governor, Ransom was not renominated by his party. The Democrats were split on the slavery issue and Ransom was firmly opposed to it. He returned to Kalamazoo and served as a member of the Board of Regents of the University of Michigan (1850-52). He was elected to one term in the Michigan House of Representatives (1853-54).

The family enjoyed farm life, but the town was encroaching on their acreage so Ransom sold it for $12,000 in gold. This was considered a fortune at that time, but within a few years his land had been resold in plots to the tune of $100,000.

Ransom went into partnership with his son, Wyllys, and invested most of his money in plank roads and a banking business. The bank was successful until the panic of 1855 and then it was forced to go into liquidation. The money he'd advanced for construction of the Kalamazoo and Grand Rapids Plank Road was lost in litigation and through a legal technicality. The coming of the railroads played havoc with this project, too.

Having suffered such serious financial reverses and broken in health, the former Governor moved with Almira to Kansas in 1856. Their son, Wyllys, his wife, Mary, and their little boy, Arthur, who had been born in 1854, accompanied them. In 1857, President James Buchanan appointed Ransom as receiver of the public monies for the Osage land office at Fort Scott, Kansas.[7]

Their lives went on at Fort Scott, but starting out fresh at their ages must have been difficult for a couple having lived so well in Michigan. "Epaphro," as he sometimes signed his name, was one of three federal officers whose lives were threatened by pro-slavery forces on the Kansas frontier.[8]

Wyllys and Mary had another son, William, born on October 27, 1857. Two years later Ransom died at the age of 62, on November 11, 1859. The following January his family brought his body back for a funeral in Kalamazoo and he was buried in the Mountain Home Cemetery.

Almira remained in their home at Fort Scott. Wyllys and Mary had another son, Robert Burns, born there on January 2, 1861. Wyllys went off to the Civil War and returned with the commission of major. Almira's daughter, Antoinette, had married George J. Clark in Kalamazoo in 1854, but later moved to Fort Scott to be with her mother.

Almira was living with Antoinette when she died on March 17, 1877. Her body was brought back to the home of her grandson, Arthur, a doctor in Kalamazoo. The funeral was held at St. Luke's Church and she was buried beside the Governor in the Ransom plot of the Mountain Home Cemetery.[9] ❖

This was the Ransom homestead in Kalamazoo until Governor Ransom sold it in 1851, along with the entire Ransom farm for $12,000 in gold.   Kalamazoo Public Library/Kalamazoo Gazette

❖ Historical Note

At the turn of the century the sale of the Ransom house, built in 1847, was offered for use as a museum to the city for $6,000. But interest in a museum dwindled and the purchase was not made. Part of the house was rebuilt to form an apartment building at 509 South Burdick Street. Another part of the house and barns were moved to the corner of John Street and Walnut Street. In 1985, the original location, where the Kalamazoo Gazette now stands, was registered as a Michigan Historical Site and a marker was placed there in 1987.

❖ Sarah S. McClelland ❖

Wife of

Governor Robert McClelland

1851 to March 8, 1853

Described as a "beautiful and estimable lady," Elizabeth Sarah Sabin was married to Robert McClelland by the Rector of Trinity Episcopal Church in Monroe on June 20, 1837.[1]

Sarah, as she was called, was born June 29, 1814, in Pittsfield, Massachusetts, and raised in Williamstown, Massachusetts. When they married, McClelland was a successful lawyer and seven years her senior.

He had arrived in Monroe in the summer or fall of 1833, from Pennsylvania. He practiced for two years with John Quincy Adams before opening his own office. He then served as a member of the 1835 Michigan Constitutional Convention that formed the first constitution of the state.[2]

Two years after their marriage McClelland was elected to the Michigan House of Representatives, and in 1840 the couple purchased a house in Monroe that had been built in 1835. It had a Greek Revival facade, somewhat unusual for Michigan in its use of pilasters rather than free standing columns. They built a one-story addition on the west end of the house for use as a library by McClelland.

The library was probably needed for a quiet place to study, since the McClellands had six children during these years. After serving in the Michigan Legislature, McClelland was elected as a U.S. Congressman and served three terms, from 1843 to 1849.[3]

McClelland was a delegate to the 1850 Michigan Constitutional Convention and was elected governor in 1851. This was a one-year term, as specified in the newly adopted constitution, but he was re-elected in 1852 to a two-year term. He resigned in March of 1853 when President Franklin Pierce appointed him Secretary of the Interior.

By now, the McClelland children were older, so they sold their house in Monroe and moved to Washington, D.C. for four years.[4] When they returned, they settled in Detroit and lived at the Michigan Exchange Hotel on the corner of Shelby Street and Jefferson Avenue. It was considered the most elegant place to live at the time.

Robert McClelland
State Archives

30

Fletcher Webster, the son of Daniel Webster, lived there with his wife, and the couples were good friends. Whenever the famous orator-politician visited Detroit on business, he also spent time with the McClellands.[5]

Continuing his interest in government, McClelland served as a delegate from Wayne County to the 1867 Michigan Constitutional Convention in Lansing. He died on August 30, 1880.

Sarah died May 9, 1887, when she was 72 years old. They are both buried in Elmwood Cemetery of Detroit. At the time of her death, only two of their six children were living. One of these was a daughter named Augusta. Augusta married George Nexsen Brady in December of 1865, in Detroit, and died on April 22, 1909. The couple had two children, Robert McClelland Brady and Mary A. Brady. Mary married Rear Admiral Robert M. Berry of the U.S. Navy.[6]

Augusta was the great-great aunt of Donald M. D. Thurber, who lives in Grosse Pointe today. ❖

Governor Robert and Sarah McClelland lived in this house with their family until he was elected governor and they moved to Detroit. Located at 47 East Elm Street in Monroe, it is privately owned. It is on the National Register and was in the 1936 Historic American Buildings Survey.   *Monroe County Historical Commission*

❖ Anna Marilla Ferrand ❖ Stewart Parsons

Wife of

Acting Governor Andrew Parsons

1853 and 1854

Anna Marilla Ferrand, called Annie but later known as Marilla, was the second wife of Andrew Parsons and was First Lady during his year and nearly ten months as acting governor. Historical records are careful to point out that he was an "acting" governor, although he served virtually an entire term. Governor Robert McClelland had resigned to become Secretary of the Interior in March of 1853, only two months after his re-election.

Marilla was born on December 13, 1820, to a politically-oriented family in Cayuga County, New York. Her mother was Fanny Marilla Shaw and her father was the Honorable Bethuel Farrand. Ferrand had been raised by an uncle who was a member of state and national councils for 36 years.

Ferrand and Fanny had four children before her death in 1821; Lucius S., Jacob S., and twins, Anna Marilla and Bethuel Clinton. In 1822, he remarried and had three sons. In the fall of 1825, Ferrand brought his wife and seven children to Michigan and settled in Ann Arbor. Two years later he was elected the first probate judge in Washtenaw County.

Courtesy of Joanne C. Nelson

Marilla was only 4 years old at the time she traveled from New York to Ann Arbor with her family. She could recall years later "many incidents of the long journey, and that they went over the Indian trail to Ann Arbor… then a village of log huts and Indians were frequent visitors to its stores."[1]

When she was 19, Marilla married 25 year-old Harlow S. Stewart, an attorney from Ypsilanti. They lived in Dexter where a daughter, Sarah Caroline, was born on November 10, 1840. Another daughter, Mary, and a son, Charles Ferrand Stewart, were born before moving to Shiawassee County. Charles was born in 1842 near Ann Arbor.[2] The record is not clear regarding Mary, but Marilla's husband died on January 28, 1848, and left her with three small children.

Marilla married Andrew Parsons a year after the death of her husband and six months after the death of his wife. Parsons had come to Michigan when he was 17 years old, from Hoosick, New York, where he had been born on July 22, 1817. He had married Elvira Rowe on January 20, 1839, but she died ten years later and left him with two children: Daniel, born in 1839; and Esther, born 1842. Marilla's children; Sarah, Mary, and Charles, were also within that age range.

By the time the 1850 U.S. Federal Census was taken on August 13, Parsons was 33 years old and Marilla, age 29, had a full house with five children. Later they had two children together. A daughter, Elvina (called Ellie or Etta), was born in 1851,[3] and a son, Andrew E., on February 24, 1855. Andrew was born less than two months after Parsons left the Office of Governor and only four months before he died at age 37.

At the time Marilla married Parsons, he had been involved in politics on local and state levels for several years. He had been elected to the Michigan Senate in 1846 and had served as prosecuting attorney in Shiawassee County in 1848. In 1852 he was elected lieutenant governor, and when Governor McClelland resigned two months after his re-election, Parsons became acting governor on March 7, 1853.

As was customary in those days, Marilla's activity as First Lady was primarily keeping the home fires burning and raising the children. But the state capital had been moved to Lansing in 1847, about 35 miles from Corunna, where they resided. This shorter distance allowed the couple to spend more time together than previous governors who had to travel from Kalamazoo, Constantine, or Detroit to the capital. Also, with her family background, it can be assumed she was familiar with the political scene and supported her husband when he refused to bend to the demands of large business interests… the railroads in particular.

After he went out of office as governor on January 3, 1855, Parsons served in the Michigan House of Representatives for the 1855 session, but was in feeble health by the time he returned home to Corunna. He died on June 6, 1855, and was buried in the Pinetree Cemetery beside his first wife. His tombstone is a modest marble slab with the state seal engraved on it; the only Michigan Governor's tombstone to be so marked.[4]

Marilla, left with an infant and the other children ranging in age to 18 years old, took in at least one boarder to survive. On January 8, 1857, Robert Ferguson Gulick wrote that he was "boarding with Mrs. P., the widow of the late Governor… with her are six children …" He continued, "It is a good place to board and Mrs. P. is a pious Christian lady and has better common sense than to want to marry me."[5] (Gulick later married her daughter, Sarah Stewart.)

In June of 1862, Marilla married George C. Holmes in Corunna,[3] but he disappeared from the scene within a year and she retook the name of Parsons. She celebrated her 80th birthday while a resident of the Thompson Home for Old Ladies in Detroit, and died there after a fall that fractured her hip, on October 27, 190✿. She was buried in Woodmere Cemetery of Detroit.[6]

Andrew Parsons
State Archives

❖ Mary W. Bingham ❖

Wife of

Governor Kinsley S. Bingham

1855 through 1858

hen Mary Warden arrived in Green Oak from Scotland with her parents, Robert and Mary Alexander Warden, she was anxious to see the other members of their family who had preceded them on the long journey overseas.

The earlier arrivals included her sisters, Margaret and Janet, and a brother, Robert Warden. They had settled briefly in Camillus, New York, where Margaret met Kinsley Scott Bingham, who had been born on December 16, 1808. The couple was married in Camillus in 1833 and all four of them drove by horse and wagon through Canada to Michigan.[1]

Bingham and his brother-in-law, Robert, jointly purchased 400 acres of land in Green Oak Township, Livingston County. They began clearing the land and building a double log house. The country was described as being on the border of civilization with wolves howling outside cabin walls. It was here on May 28, 1834, that Margaret gave birth to a son, Kinsley Warden. She died four days later.

This left Janet to take care of the baby. She later married Alonzo W. Olds and little Kinsley W. was taken to Marcellus to live with them.

During this time, Bingham became active in local politics. He served as a justice of the peace and postmaster under the territorial government and was elected in 1836 to the Michigan Legislature. When Mary, who had been born in 1812, arrived with her parents from Scotland, they all lived in the double log house. Mary and Bingham were attracted to each other and a life with the ambitious lawmaker appealed to her. Despite the fact that her mother opposed Mary getting married to her dead sister's husband, she and Bingham were wed on June 10, 1839, in Green Oak.[2]

The couple had a son, James, born to them in 1840. They then asked to have young Kinsley W. sent back to them from Marcellus. A cousin recalled the family story years later, "He (Kinsley W.) was 6 or 7 years old when they asked to have him sent home. An opportunity came to send him to Ann Arbor and from there he had a chance to ride to Green Oak. It happened to be town meeting day and Kinsley was dropped off there. The lad attracted much attention and Uncle Kinsley engaged him in conversation and said, 'You are a pretty bright boy. Whose boy are you?' He was astonished to be told, 'I am your boy.'"[3]

Bingham's political career continued to progress as he was re-elected to the Michigan Legislature four times. Meanwhile, Mary stayed home with the two children in Green Oak and corresponded with her husband while he was at the capital.

Mary wrote in a letter on March 27, 1841, "The time passes with me pretty fast. I am busy sewing when I find time. I will require about three yards of fine linen to make up the shirts that I have on hand, and you must also bring a loaf of sugar."[4]

In 1846 and again in 1848, Bingham was elected a U.S. Congressman. Mary made the trip with him to Washington in November of 1849. In a letter home she wrote, "We had the company of General (Lewis) Cass and Governor (Alpheus) Felch all the way from Syracuse, and a more agreeable, unassuming old gentleman than the General is, I never saw." Later, in a letter on December 11, she commented, "I have not called at the White House yet, but think I will next Tuesday."[5]

When the Republican party was organized "under the oaks" in Jackson on July 6, 1854, Bingham was nominated for governor and was elected that fall to the office. He was re-elected in 1856.

Mary, as usual, remained at home during his gubernatorial years. But she was influential in her own Scottish way. When a mother from New York State came to Michigan to plead for her only son's release from the Jackson prison, she was unsuccessful. He'd been sentenced to five years for larceny and neither the warden nor the chaplain would recommend a pardon. The woman took the train to Ann Arbor and then walked 17 miles to arrive at Governor Bingham's home at 11:00 p.m.

Mary invited the woman in, had her stay the night, and heard her plight. The next morning the Governor signed the orders for a pardon. When asked about it later, Bingham was quoted as saying, "If your wife had joined in her plea as mine did … you would have yielded."[6]

During the two terms Bingham was elected to the U.S. Senate, 1859 and 1861, Mary accompanied him to President Abraham Lincoln's first inaugural ball. She wore a dress made from silk material her husband selected and bought while on a trip to New York. Its green stripes and rose garlands were somewhat startling to the conservative Mary and she was a little disappointed, said her niece, Mrs. William C. Stevens, years later.

Kinsley S. Bingham
State Archives

Mary never wore the dress after the ball. The Civil War broke out the summer of 1861. Their son, James, joined the state normal volunteers and was transferred to the U.S. Army. Bingham died suddenly at their home in Green Oak on October 5, 1861. The following year, in November of 1862, James died in the service at Bardstown, Kentucky. Mary wore black until her death on Christmas Day, December 25, 1882. She was buried with the rest of her family that had been moved from a private cemetery on the Bingham farm to the old cemetery in Brighton.[7]

Kinsley W. followed his father's footsteps and was elected to the state senate, an office he held at the time of his death in June of 1908. He was survived by an adopted daughter, Mrs. August Dryer.[8] Thus neither Margaret, Mary, nor Kinsley Scott Bingham left any direct descendants. However, Bingham's sister, Caroline, had married Robert Warden in 1841, and there were several nieces and nephews. ❖

The Bingham homestead was built in 1842 on Silver Lake Road, near South Lyon. It is owned by the American Aggregate Corporation and they have turned the basement over for use by the Green Oak Historical Society.　　　　　　Green Oak Historical Society

❖ Historical Note

The Bingham house at 13270 Silver Lake Road, between Kensington (Peer) Road and Dixboro Road, near South Lyon in Green Oak Township, is now owned by the American Aggregates Corporation and used for district offices. The Corporation has turned the basement over to the Green Oak Historical Society where information regarding the Bingham family is preserved. In 1973, the house was designated and marked as a historical site by the Michigan Historical Commission.

❖ Angeolina H. Wisner ❖

Wife of

Governor Moses Wisner

1859 and 1860

Angeolina Hascall was the daughter of one of Flint's earliest pioneers and civic leaders, General C. C. Hascall. He and his wife, Nancy Rounds, had come to Detroit from New York and settled in Auburn, where Angeolina was born on March 4, 1828.[1]

Her father was called "General" due to his appointment as head of the local militia in the Toledo War. Her parents were well-to-do: owned a farm, woolen mill, store, and hotel. When she was 9 years old they moved to Flint where she was raised.

As there were few public schools in those days, Angeolina was tutored in the office of her father's store with her brother, Charles, her cousin, Martha, and another boy. As she grew into a "fair and sprightly" young lady, she met Moses Wisner, a widower with a young son, Edward M., on a visit to Pontiac where he was practicing law.[2]

After a whirlwind courtship on his part, but with some hesitancy on hers, 20 year-old Angeolina and 33 year-old Moses were married in 1848 at her parent's home in Flint. They went to live at Pine Grove, a farm he'd purchased four years earlier. Wisner continued to buy land and build until their home became a spacious country estate. It was here, in Pontiac Township, that their children were born:[3] Charles, called "Chip," was born on February 27, 1850; Frank, in September of 1854; and Jessica, on November 8, 1856. Edward, her step-son, attended Mr. Bacon's School for Boys in Detroit.

Angeolina was kept busy running a large household. She specialized in baking and won prizes at the county fair for her homemade bread. Meanwhile, Wisner attended the meeting "under the oaks" in Jackson when the Republican party was formed. He was a member of the nominating committee that selected Kinsley S. Bingham for governor.

Wisner was nominated as a representative to congress from his district on the Republican ticket, but he was defeated. In 1858, however, he was nominated for governor and won the election. It was his first and only political victory.[4] "Chip," not quite 9 years old, accompanied his father to Lansing for his inauguration. Angeolina remained at home to care for their other children and her father who was ill.

The Governor's annual salary of $1,000 was not sufficient to provide a home for the family in Lansing, so official entertaining was done at Pine Grove. Angeolina had their parlor enlarged and redecorated with new wallpaper, carpeting, and draperies. The sofa was reupholstered with black horsehair to match two small love seats. She maintained the room in the same condition the rest of her life, telling visitors, "This is the way it was when the Governor lived here."[5]

One of Angeolina's favorite memories was when she and Moses were hosts at a visit by the Prince of Wales, later King Edward VII, at the Russell House in Detroit on September 20, 1860.

Although Wisner was neither aware of the situation nor responsible for it, mismanagement of funds by the state treasurer during the time he was governor was revealed. This may have influenced his decision not to run for a second term.

Wisner returned to Pine Grove and his law practice until the beginning of the Civil War. In July 1862, he was appointed by Governor Austin Blair to recruit and train the 22nd Michigan Regiment of Infantry. Colonel Wisner departed with 997 men on September 4 for combat in Kentucky. In November he became ill with typhoid fever and a month later, when his condition worsened, Angeolina hurried to be with him. He had been moved to a house in Lexington and she was at his bedside when he died on January 5, 1863.

Only 35 years old at the time of Wisner's death, Angeolina was faced with raising their three children, all under 14 years of age. She was frail, but intelligent with a good business head, and managed to maintain Pine Grove with its 185 acres. Three years after the death of her husband, their second son, Frank, died following a brief illness at the age of 13, on October 5, 1867.

Angeolina never remarried. Neither her step-son, Edward, nor "Chip" had children, so the Wisner name was not carried on directly. Jessica Wisner (Clark), however, married and had a daughter, Florence Clark (Wallace), before her death at age 50.

When Angeolina died at the age of 77 in 1905, she was buried beside her husband in the family plot in Oak Hill Cemetery, Pontiac. Her last wish was that Pine Grove be preserved. For 40 years her only granddaughter, Florence, and her family maintained the home.

Moses Wisner
State archives

In 1945, Pine Grove was sold to the Oakland County Historical Foundation as a center for the Pioneer and Historical Society, and Angeolina's request was fulfilled. It has become a state and national historical site.[6] ❖

Pine Grove, the Wisner home northwest of downtown Pontiac, was built in 1850. It contains many original furnishings and is now headquarters for the Oakland County Pioneer Historical Society.   Oakland County Pioneer and Historical Society

❖ Sarah H. Blair ❖

Wife of

Governor Austin Blair

1861 through 1864

Sarah Louisa Horton Ford Blair was First Lady during the Civil War years and she devoted much of her time to helping young soldiers camped in Jackson as well as throughout the state. Her work for the relief of the sick and wounded in hospitals and prisons of the South was "constant and great." She was also credited with ably assisting her husband, Austin Blair, the War Governor of Michigan.[1]

Sarah was born in Waterloo, New York, on August 11, 1824, and was among the pioneers of Jackson County, Michigan. She was the 25 year-old widow of Amos Ford when she married 30 year-old Blair on January 17, 1849, in Jackson.

Blair, who was born in Tompkins County, New York, on February 8, 1818, had been admitted to the bar in Tioga County. He moved to Jackson, Michigan, when he was 23 and set up a law practice. In February of 1841, he married Persis Lyman, and they moved to Eaton Rapids. A year later, a daughter, Gertrude, was born to them on February 17, 1842. The infant died when she was 7 months old, on September 12 of that year, and Persis died the following January at the age of 24.

Although Blair served as Eaton County Clerk in 1843, he resigned early in 1844 and moved back to Jackson. It is believed that the tragic death of his wife and child influenced his decision.

Within two years, Blair had been elected to the Michigan Legislature, and in May of 1846, he married his second wife, Elizabeth Pratt. A year later, she also died at the age of 24, on April 28, 1847, and their infant son, James Hunter, died when he was 4 months old.

Austin Blair
State Archives

Two years later, Blair married Sarah Ford, on February 16, 1849. He must have been very nervous when their first son, George Henry, was born on April 10, a year later. But both Sarah and Baby George survived. His birth was followed by that of: a daughter, Nelly, on October 10, 1851; Charles Austin, on April 10, 1854; Frederick J., on December 15, 1860; and Austin True, on January 27, 1864. Austin True was born while Blair was governor. Nelly died when she was 10 months old, but the three boys survived their parents (George Henry Blair died in 1903).[2]

With family life more settled and growing, Austin and Sarah built a 24-room house in Jackson two years after their marriage. Blair continued his career in politics. He was a leader in the meeting "under the oaks," when the Republican party was formed in 1854, and was elected to the state senate for a two-year term beginning in 1855.

By the time Blair was inaugurated as governor on New Year's Day in 1861, the Civil War was imminent, and in April he was asked to raise a regiment of ten companies from Michigan. Although the legislature had authorized the raising of troops, it had not appropriated the necessary funds. Blair raised between $81,000 to $100,000 through donations from private sources and accomplished the mission.

Sarah helped her husband while the war efforts were being carried on. She was a woman of strong vitality and ardent patriotism. She endeared herself to the soldiers by her kind deeds. During the encampment of the 20th and 26th Michigan Infantry on the Marvin farm in Jackson "she filled with almost motherly love the hearts of many young patriots who had left their homes to fight for the nation's honor."[3]

After the war, the Blairs added a drawing room to their home which extended the entire left side of the house. It was built to accommodate the huge gilt and marble console mirrors given to the Governor by officers of the 10th and 11th Michigan Cavalry.

A picket fence surrounded the estate of several acres and great pines stood in the yard. Sarah and Austin had planted them between 1850 and 1860. Their grand-daughter, Nellie Blair Greene, later described her feelings when she came to visit.

"One arrived, after a long journey in a slow train from Lansing; either drove... with much pomp in a curious vehicle known as a "hack" or... with even more pomp... in the family carriage behind the two old black horses with grinning black Joe on the seat, around through the back streets, to Trail and then up the long hill to Grandfather's house.

"It was a never-ending thrill, to a strange child, that first glimpse of the old house, framed by its beautiful trees, with the sun shining upon the old-fashioned garden, and Grandmother waiting there by the corner nearest the drawing room where the drive curved around towards the barn.

"Over the porch was an Indian pipe-vine, where we once found a little queer doll belonging to some former generation... Aunt Nelly, so they said, the little girl who died in 1852. There was not much left of the doll; Grandmother took it away into her room, and stayed there for a long time, very quietly."[4]

Still active on behalf of the troops after the war, Sarah became the first president of the Jackson Ladies Soldiers and Sailors Monument Association when it was formed on June 18, 1867. It was an organization to collect funds to erect monuments in honor of veterans.[5]

When Blair left the governorship after two terms, he had a law office in Jackson and was assisted by his son, Charles.[6] The Governor's salary was $1,000 a year at that time and he had contributed a good share of his income to the war effort. He died on August 6, 1894, after several years of a declining law practice, lack of money, and failing health.[7]

Sarah survived Blair by three years. She had been in fair health until the death of her husband but then began going downhill. A friend of the family told the following story:

"When Sarah Blair had been very sick and unconscious for several days, her family gathered in her room... and among them her three daughters-in-law, all eagerly awaiting her first word. She tried hard to speak, to make them understand what was on her mind, for it was plain something vital was at stake, something was worrying her.

The Blair Homestead. Jackson Centennial 1829-1929 Official Program

"The wife of her oldest son thought perhaps she wanted to make her will; the next believed she wished to tell them something... a vision, possibly of her first husband, Amos Ford; the third said she knew she wanted a minister, or someone to pray for her.

"Finally Sarah spoke... with great difficulty, but clearly enough. And this is what she said: 'Pears!... In the dark cupboard... forgot them... rotting!'"[8]

Sarah died July 1, 1897, and was buried in the Blair plot, Mount Evergreen Cemetery, Jackson. Her name is engraved on the tombstone as Sarah Louesa. Here, in addition to Governor Blair, are his three wives and the two infants by his first two wives. Blair and Sarah's son, Charles A., who died in 1912, his wife, Effie, who died in 1944, and their two children; Emma Louise and Walter Guy, who both died in 1886, are also buried there.

A year after Blair's death, the Michigan Legislature appropriated funds for a memorial statue of him, which still stands in front of the Capitol in Lansing. One hundred and twenty years after he served as governor, Michigan Historical Markers were placed at his former house in Eaton Rapids and in a park in Jackson which was re-named in his honor. ❖

❖ **Historical Note**

In 1913, the Governor Austin Blair Estate on Lansing Avenue in Jackson, was purchased for the site of Mercy Hospital and construction begun in 1917. Ten years later, a bronze marker commemorating the site of the home of Austin Blair was placed almost on the spot where Sarah's garden had once bloomed, by the Sarah Treat Prudden Chapter, DAR. It was assumed that the house had been razed.

A section of the Blair House in Jackson, purchased in 1989 and restored by Mr. and Mrs. James D. Cannon.

Courtesy of Donna Cannon

In 1931 the *Jackson Tribune* reported locating a major portion of the old Blair homestead that had been moved to 1301 Deyo Street. In 1992, Donna Cannon contacted the author to say she and her husband, James, had purchased the old Blair house in 1989 when it was in a dilapidated state, condemned, and scheduled for demolition. It is located just to the north of where the hospital building stood and had been used as housing for nurses at the hospital.

Apparently, this portion of the Blair house had been moved only a short distance. The Cannons have restored it so the big porch is still there and the interior, with the original staircase, beautiful woodwork, and third floor attic, is as it was when the Blairs lived there.

Ironically, Mercy Hospital was sold in 1975 and has been razed.

❖ Mary Ann S. Crapo ❖

Wife of

Governor Henry H. Crapo

1865 through 1868

ichigan, as well as the nation, might not be the same today if Mary Ann Slocum hadn't recognized that Henry Howland Crapo was an extraordinary person. Despite initial opposition by her parents, she married Crapo and he became a governor, their son became a U.S. Congressman, and their grandson founded General Motors Corporation.

The Slocum family was a prosperous one living at Barney's Joy on Slocum's Neck in Massachusetts. They were Friends, as the English Quakers were called.

Mary Ann, born June 9, 1805, was unusually well prepared to be the wife of a public figure. Her education at the Friend's School in Providence, Rhode Island, provided her with the social finish expected in that era.

When Mary Ann met Henry Crapo, he was a young school teacher with a meager income, but great determination. Born in Dartmouth, Massachusetts, in 1804, he had struggled, virtually penniless, to become a teacher in a nearby district. He had a good family heritage, however. He was a descendant of Resolved White, a member of the original 1620 Mayflower Company.

Mary Ann's father frowned upon their attraction because Crapo was not a Friend, owned no property, and was not in a profession that promised much of a future for a young girl raised in prosperous circumstances.

With characteristic persistence, Crapo continued his suit, including one to win over Mary Ann's mother. With her help, he won the father's approval and the couple were married on June 9, 1825, in Dartmouth, Massachusetts. Due to their strained financial situation, Mary Ann continued living with her parents at Barney's Joy for several years after their marriage.[1]

During this time, two of their children were born. Crapo "was accustomed to walk home on Saturday to see his family, returning on Sunday in order to be ready for school Monday morning."[2] The walk, for a good part of the time, was 20 miles each way. But this enabled them to save their money and through investments primarily in real estate he became highly successful.

By 1856 the family had ten children, nine of them daughters, and were living in resplendent circumstances. Crapo was keenly interested in horticulture and real estate. He had invested so heavily in Michigan pine lands that he decided they should move to Flint to tend their holdings.

Mary Ann must have called on all the "strength of character, courage, hopefulness and devotion" ascribed to her, when she left her comfortable life to come to Michigan. Her grandson, Henry H. Crapo II, later wrote that she had given up "a splendid home in New Bedford, Massachusetts, with its trees and gardens, farms and nurseries," to move to unfamiliar surroundings. At the age of 51, she left many relatives, friends and three of her children to go west and pioneer.

"Bravely she put aside her fears, graciously and steadfastly she helped her husband in his adventurous scheme, establish a new home in the wilderness and make new friends, with an ever-increasing pride in her beloved's achievements."[3]

Two of the children who did not come to Michigan were Rebecca Folger (Mrs. William Clark Durant) and their only son, William W. Crapo. He was for many years a member of Congress from New Bedford. Their other children were Mary (Mrs. John Orrell), Sarah (Mrs. Alphonso Ross), Rhoda (Mrs. James C. Willson), Henrietta (Mrs. Ferris F. Hyatt), Lucy (Mrs. Humphrey Howland Crapo Smith), Lydia, who died unmarried in 1861, Emma (Mrs. Harrow Page Cristy), and Wilhelmina (Mrs. Charles W. Clifford).[4]

Within a relatively short time after arriving in Flint, Crapo became a lumber baron and more than regained his financial standing. He contributed to Flint's lumber boom and at one time had as many as five lumber mills in operation simultaneously. The Flint and Holly Railroad, built by Governor Crapo and his friends, linked this area to the rest of the country.[5]

Crapo was elected mayor of Flint in 1860, to a senate seat during 1863 and 1864, and in 1865 was sworn in as governor of Michigan. During his two terms in office he spent much of his time in Lansing while Mary Ann tended their fine home in Flint. She also managed their home and 1,385 acre farm in Swartz Creek, west of Flint, which became famous for its Hereford cattle.

The couple was especially fond of William "Billy" Crapo Durant, son of their daughter, Rebecca. She did not move to Michigan until 1872, after the death of her father, but they had visited often. Billy spent much time on the Swartz Creek farm as a boy and was influenced by the strong character of his grandfather. When he was grown, he created General Motors, the largest industrial corporation in the world, acquiring and losing several fortunes.

Henry Crapo
State Archives

45

Crapo died in July of 1869, less than a year after leaving office as governor. When Mary Ann died six years later, February of 1875, their estate was estimated at between one-half to one million dollars.[6] They were both buried in Flint.

A school in Flint was named for Mary Ann Crapo and her portrait was presented to the school in 1976. In 1980, a park was named for Governor Crapo on the site of his Holly lumberyard and a Michigan Historical Marker was placed there in his honor. ❖

The Crapo family about 1855. Front row (from left): Henrietta (Mrs. Ferris F. Hyatt), Rhoda (Mrs. James C. Willson), Wilhelmina (Mrs. Charles W. Clifford), Governor Crapo, Mary Crapo, Emma (Mrs. Harrow Page Cristy), Lucy (Mrs. Humphrey Howland Crapo Smith), Lydia (who died unmarried in 1861). Back row (from left): Mary (Mrs. John Orrell), William Wallace Crapo, Rebecca (Mrs. William Clark Durant), Sarah (Mrs. Alphonso Ross). The Flint Journal

❖ Sibyl L. Baldwin ❖

Wife of

Governor Henry P. Baldwin

1869 through 1872

Sibyl Baldwin was one of the most prominent club women and society leaders in Detroit. She was described as wealthy, accomplished and a most charming woman. She also obviously had a mind of her own. Twenty years after Governor Baldwin's death, Sibyl married a man about 35 years her junior.

Henry Porter Baldwin, born on February 22, 1814, in Rhode Island, was in the mercantile business when he married his first wife, Harriet M. Day of Pawtucket, in 1835. The couple came to Detroit in the spring of 1838.

While he was establishing a successful shoe and boot business and becoming an influential banker, they had four children: Ella, Florence, Frederick, and Jeanie. They all died in infancy or while young, except Jeanie, who became Mrs. Percy B. Rose, and survived Baldwin.[1]

Baldwin was elected to the Michigan Senate in 1860 and on January 24, 1865, Harriet died. Almost two years later, on November 21, 1866, he married his second wife, Sibyl Lambard or Sibyle Lombard. Sibyl was 25 years younger than Baldwin, having been born on February 24, 1839, and they had three daughters: Sybil, Katharine, and Marie.[2]

Burton

Sibyl became First Lady of Michigan when Baldwin was elected governor in 1869 and re-elected in 1871. In Lansing, the Capitol was housed in the frame statehouse it had occupied since the state government was moved from Detroit in 1848. The legislature authorized funds for a new building upon Baldwin's recommendation and contracts were let for its construction during his administration.[3]

Upon completing his two terms as governor, the Baldwins returned to Detroit and built a mansion on the northwest corner of Fort Street and Cass Avenue. The site was where General Lewis Cass had a frame house built upon his return from ministerial duties in France in 1843.

Henry P. Baldwin
State Archives

In the central entrance hall was a grand staircase. Opening off the hall were large high-ceilinged rooms, their walls lined with the Governor's collection of paintings. It was here that former Governor and Mrs. Baldwin held a reception for President and Mrs. Rutherford B. Hayes and General W. T. Sherman.[4]

Baldwin and Sibyl were active in the St. John's Episcopal Church, which was founded and heavily funded by him through the years. Although Baldwin had returned to private business after leaving the governorship, he accepted an appointment in 1879 by Governor Charles Croswell to fill a vacancy in the U.S. Senate, created by the death of Zachariah Chandler. He served 15 months, but lost his bid for the post in the next election. Baldwin died on December 31, 1892 and was buried in Elmwood Cemetery of Detroit.

The Baldwin mansion in downtown Detroit where President Rutherford B. Hayes and General W. T. Sherman were entertained by Governor and Sibyl Baldwin.   *Detroit Historical Museum*

Sibyl, who was 53 at the time of Baldwin's death, remained a widow for 20 years. Their three daughters all married and moved to New York, and eventually she went to live with one of them. Katharine had married Walter Bliss, son of Cornelius N. Bliss, Secretary of the Interior under President William McKinley; Sibyl became Mrs. Sibyl B. Wright; and Marie became Mrs. Willis Terry.[5]

Sibyl loved to travel and as she grew older it was presumed that she "felt the need of a protector in order that she might safely and comfortably pursue her bent in that direction." She married Francis de Salles Carroll, and later, when they were house hunting in Pasadena, California, a newspaper featured a story about them; "Love Bridges Gap of Years. Wife Seventy, Husband is in His Early Thirties."[6]

When Sibyl died of pneumonia at age 83 in her New York home on April 24, 1922, a Detroit newspaper carried this report: "The late Mrs. Sybil de Salles Carroll, widow of former Governor Henry P. Baldwin, and who at 70 years of age startled the old aristocracy of Detroit by marrying a youthful English clergyman, bequeathed $5,000 to St. John's Episcopal church, this city, in her will."[7]

According to the report, she left the same amount to a home for poor and indigent women in Augusta, Maine, but there was no mention in the will of Carroll. Her three grandchildren were to receive $500 each and the balance of the estate was to be divided among her three daughters.

Sibyl's body was returned to Detroit and she was buried in Elmwood Cemetery beside her husband, former Governor Baldwin. Their beautiful mansion was torn down in 1943. ❖

❖ Frances N. Bagley ❖

Wife of

Governor John J. Bagley

1873 through 1876

Frances Elizabeth Newberry and John Judson Bagley were married in Dubuque, Iowa, on January 16, 1855. She returned to Detroit with him where he owned a tobacco manufacturing business.

Frances, born March 4, 1833, was the daughter of Reverend Samuel Newberry and Mary Ann Sergeant. Reverend Newberry, a pioneer missionary and Presbyterian clergyman of Michigan, had been active in promoting an educational program in the state.

Bagley had come to Constantine at the age of eight with his family from New York where he had been born July 24, 1832. When he was 14, he moved to Owosso for two years and in 1847 he left to begin work in a tobacco factory in Detroit. He started his own tobacco manufacturing business in 1853 and it became one of the largest of its kind in the West.[1]

He was appointed one of the first commissioners of the Detroit Police Force by Governor Henry Crapo in 1865 and served for six years. Then he made a bid for the governorship.

Frances had eight children during these years; Florence, John N., Frances, Margaret, Olive, Katherine, Paul Frederick, and Helen. Seven of them were living when her husband took office as governor.[2] He was one of few early governors to reside in Lansing during the legislative sessions (most of them stayed in rented hotel rooms), so Frances was generally on hand for state ceremonies.

Continuing her family's interest in education, Frances was very active in forming educational groups for women. She organized the Women's Club in Detroit, one in Lansing, and others throughout the state. Harriet A. Tenny, state librarian, and Lucinda Stone, of Kalamazoo, were good friends of hers and all three were intent on improving the lot of women.[3]

Frances undoubtedly influenced the Governor along these lines, especially for an improved educational system for children. His improvements in institutions for delinquent and indigent children were such that they were regarded as one of the chief accomplishments during his administration. He reorganized the Boys' Reformatory in Lansing to make it more of a school and less of a prison; and developed the State Public School for Dependent Children in Coldwater for wards of the state.

A memorial fountain on the lawn of State Public School on U.S. 27 in Coldwater, was "Presented in 1878 by Governor Bagley and wife in memory of their daughter, Kittie," according to the 1931 Spring Edition of the *Michigan History Magazine,* published by the Michigan

John J. Bagley
State Archives

51

Historical Commission. It is assumed that Kittie was Katherine and the child that died before he took office as governor.

After his second term, Bagley returned to his business affairs in Detroit. He and Frances had an elegant home there where friends were always welcome. He was a large man who found his greatest happiness in his home with his family and was said to never permit business problems to enter.[4]

Bagley died on July 27, 1881, and Frances died February 7, 1898. They were both buried in Woodmere Cemetery of Detroit. ❖

The Bagley's residence in Detroit, built in 1869.

❖ Elizabeth M. Croswell ❖

Wife of

Governor Charles M. Croswell

1877 through 1880

Elizabeth Musgrave married Governor Charles Miller Croswell after he'd been re-elected in 1878, just prior to his taking office for his second term. He had been a widower for ten years.

Croswell, whose parents and only sister had died when he was 7 years old, came to Adrian from New York State with an uncle in 1837, at the age of 12. As a young man he was appointed Deputy Clerk of Lenawee County and continued holding political offices for most of his life.

He married his first wife, Lucy M. Eddy of Adrian, in February 1852, and they had five children, but only three survived; two daughters and a son. Lucy died on December 13, 1868, while in her mid-twenties. She fell down the full length of the stairway in their home, with their young baby girl in her arms. Although she lived only into the next day, the baby survived.[1] Lucy's parents came and lived with the children for the next 12 years.[2]

Lenawee County Historical Society, Inc.

Croswell, who had served three terms as a state senator, was president of the 1867 Michigan Constitutional Convention. Joseph Musgrave from Eaton County was one of the delegates and it is assumed that he was Elizabeth's father since she was born in Eaton County about 1822. Croswell and Elizabeth could have met while the convention was taking place in Lansing or while Musgrave and Croswell were both serving in the state legislature.

Elizabeth was a student at Olivet College when they married and was in the same age bracket as his daughters. She was described as "one of the most beautiful and accomplished young ladies of Lansing," and had a penchant for roses. Croswell was 52 years old at the time.[3]

After completing his second term as governor, Croswell returned to Adrian where he was president of the Lenawee County Savings Bank and bought a majority interest in the Opera House which is the Croswell Opera

Charles Croswell
State Archive

House today. He died six years after leaving office, on December 13, 1886. Three months after his death the couple's only child was born, Salliehicks Croswell, named after his mother, Sallie Hicks Croswell.

Elizabeth lived in the Croswell house for two or three years and later moved to Washington, D.C., where she became known as the "Lady of the Roses." Twelve years after the death of Croswell, she married her second husband, Thomas Merrill, a wealthy lumberman from Duluth, Minnesota. Their wedding, held in the Croswell house, was notable for its lavish decorations. The walls were draped with cheesecloth and covered with American Beauty roses at an estimated cost of $500.[4]

Although she moved with her husband to Duluth, and to what might have been a carefree life, she faced another tragedy. Her daughter, Salliehicks, was a diabetic and died when she was 16 years old.

Elizabeth had another daughter, Marie, by her second husband, Thomas Merrill.

When Elizabeth died in 1927 in Duluth, she left the Croswell house and an endowment to the Lucy Wolcott Barnum Chapter of the Daughters of the American Revolution in Adrian. DAR members have preserved the "Governor's House" which has been named a State Historical Site and is listed on the National Register of Historic Places.

The only living descendant of Governor Croswell is Priscilla Croswell Grew, Ph.D. of Lincoln, Nebraska. Dr. Grew is the great-granddaughter of Croswell and his first wife, Lucy M. Eddy Croswell. ❖

This Greek Revival house of Governor Charles and Elizabeth Croswell has been restored in Adrian by the Lucy Wolcott Barnum Chapter of DAR.　　　　*State Archives*

❖ Lucy P. Jerome ❖

Wife of

Governor David H. Jerome

1881 and 1882

David Jerome and Lucy Amelia Peck were married in 1859, while he was in the lumber operation and hardware business in Saginaw.

Lucy was the daughter of Edward W. and Lucy Frost Peck of Pontiac, Oakland County, and was born in 1834.[1] Her mother died when she was 6 years old and her father remarried. He was in the lumber business and was very influential in the area all his life. He served as a delegate from Oakland County to the First Convention of Assent, September 26-28, 1836 in Ann Arbor.[1]

Being raised in a family active in the political process while Michigan was gaining admission to the Union, gave Lucy a good understanding of government. This undoubtedly helped her adjust to the role of First Lady in later years.

When Lucy was 24 or 25, she married David Howell Jerome, who had been born on November 17, 1829, and the couple had three children; two of them died while infants. Their surviving son, Thomas Spencer Jerome, became a member of the legal profession in Detroit.[2]

Historical Society of Saginaw County

Not much can be learned about Lucy's activities while Jerome was governor, but in 1885 she was chosen as temporary chairman of the preliminary meeting of the Saginaw Reading Club. The Jerome women were leaders in their community, as evidenced by the fact that of the 48 other women meeting at the local high school, Lucy, Calista Jerome (her mother-in-law), and Mrs. James Jerome, held committee appointments.[3]

Allaseba Bliss, wife of Aaron T. Bliss, who became Governor of Michigan 16 years later, was also one of the leaders of the club. This was only natural since the Jerome and Bliss families were related by marriage.

Horace Jerome, David's father, had come from New York and died in Detroit in 1831. He had married twice. He and his first wife had five children with the last one a son, James Henry Jerome. Horace and his second wife had eight children with the last one being David Howell Jerome. Thus, James Henry and David H. Jerome were half-brothers and seventeen years apart in age.[4]

When Aaron Bliss came to Saginaw about 1867, he formed a partnership with his brother, Dr. Lyman W. Bliss, and James Henry Jerome. James Henry had a daughter, Mary Jerome, who married Dr. Bliss and they had three children.[5]

The photograph of Lucy Jerome was found in the Portrait Gallery of Residents of Saginaw (1860-1875). It was taken before Jerome was elected governor. The numbering is incorrect, but she can be identified as she is on one side of her husband with their son, Thomas, on his other side. This montage is in the Public Libraries of Saginaw and the identification has been approved by a spokesman for the Historical Society of Saginaw County.[6]

Lucy was with her husband when he died in a sanitarium at Watkins Glen, New York on April 23, 1896, at the age of 67. She died in Detroit 11 months later on March 31, 1897, at the age of 63. They were both buried in Oak Hill Cemetery, Pontiac. Their only son, Thomas, died in his early fifties on April 12, 1914, in Capri, Italy. ❖

David H. Jerome
State Archives

❖ Harriet M. Begole ❖

Wife of

Governor Josiah W. Begole

1883 and 1884

osiah W. Begole arrived in Genesee County of the Michigan Territory from New York in 1836. A year later, Harriet A. Miles arrived in the area with her parents.

Harriet and Josiah met and their romance bloomed. The young couple was married in her family's log house, north of Flint, on April 22, 1839. It was one of the first weddings, if not the very first, to take place in the sparsely settled area and created quite a stir.

Harriet Annette was born on November 25, 1817, to Manley and Mary Cushman Miles. Some records show Connecticut as her birthplace, others show New York. However, her father had been a carriage maker in Cazenovia, New York, when the family left for Michigan. They brought their five lively daughters and two sons with them to the new territory. Miles carried on his trade in Flint and also farmed.

Harriet was active in whatever was happening in the new community right from the start, as her detailed letters to relatives back home indicate.[1]

Newly married Harriet and Josiah began housekeeping in the woods in Genesee Township and spent the next 18 years working to develop it into a 500-acre productive farm. Josiah also became a wealthy businessman and was a founder and owner of one of Flint's largest sawmills.

State archives

During this period, Harriet bore five children: Mary Cummings, William, Frank, Charles, and a daughter who died in infancy. Their eldest son, William, died as a result of wounds received in the Civil War, near Atlanta, Georgia, in 1864.

After being county treasurer for eight years, Begole was elected to the state senate in 1870. When he finished this term, he was elected as a U.S. Congressman and served during 1873 and 1874. While in Washington, D.C., he voted for issuance of large amounts of paper money and became known as a "Greenbacker." Twelve years later, in 1883, the Greenback and Democrat parties supported him as a Fusionist candidate and he was elected governor of Michigan.

Begole was 68 years old when he took office, the oldest man ever to be elected governor of Michigan. He was also the only Fusionist ever elected.

While he was busy with politics, Harriet was active in civic affairs. She was a charter member and treasurer of the Ladies' Library Association, which established Flint's first subscription library, a forerunner of today's public library system. She made the first donation toward the King's Daughters Home, a child care center, and her name was on almost every civic roster.

With Harriet's influence, Begole was involved in the work of the Flint Woman's Suffrage Association and he was a suffrage advocate during his term as governor.

The couple celebrated their 50th Wedding Anniversary in 1889. It was reported: "The marriage (had) proved a most fortunate one, and to the faithful wife of his youth, who lives to enjoy with him the comforts of an honestly earned competence, Mr. Begole ascribes largely his success in life."[2]

After his death on June 6, 1896, Begole was eulogized by Governor John T. Rich as "one of those who helped redeem our state from a wilderness." His words were equally applicable to Harriet Begole who died 15 years later on August 17, 1911. The Begoles were buried in Flint and were survived by only two of their children. They had grandchildren, however, and numerous Flint residents are descendants of this pioneer couple. ❖

Josiah W. Begole
State Archives

❖ Annette H. Alger ❖

Wife of

Governor Russell A. Alger

1885 and 1886

nnette H. Henry met Russell Alexander Alger when he moved to her hometown of Grand Rapids. He had been practicing law in Cleveland, Ohio, but decided to give it up due to failing health and try his hand in the lumber business.[1]

The eldest daughter of Honorable W. Gilmore Henry and Huldana Squire, Annette Huldana Squire Henry was born on July 29, 1840, at the home of her grandparents in New Haven, Vermont. The family moved to Grand Rapids where she met Alger. She was 19 years old when they were married on April 2, 1861, in her parent's house located in what is now downtown Grand Rapids (the *Grand Rapids Press* Building was later erected on the site).

Annette was described as a slender young woman of fair complexion, intelligent, and attractive. She was gifted with many accomplishments and a charming hostess.

Soon after their marriage Alger enlisted in the 2nd Michigan Volunteer Cavalry and left to fight in the Civil War. Alger was wounded two times in battle and established a distinguished military record.[2] He resigned in 1864 for health and personal reasons. In 1865 he was given brevet promotions to Brigadier and Major General and, according to one account, served at President Abraham Lincoln's personal orders.

When he returned from the service, Russell and Annette moved to Detroit, where he re-entered the lumber business. Although his earlier venture in lumbering had left in him debt by the time he joined the army, the economic situation was better now. He became a leading partner in several lumber companies which were very profitable. His success in the lumber companies, building railroads, and mining investments made him a multimillionaire.

Although Alger had no political experience, he was a war hero and a successful businessman. Based primarily on these qualifications, he was nominated for governor by the Republican party and won the election in 1884.

The Algers lived in Lansing some of the time during his two years as governor. Annette was considered very social and it was said she "gave class" to the position of First Lady.

Although nine children were born to the couple,[3] only six were living at the time Alger was governor. Two of their daughters, Fay, a lively brunette, and Caroline A., a rather tall girl resembling her mother, attended a seminary in the East and traveled together through Europe for a year. Their other children were Frances, Russell Jr., Fred, and Allen. Allen was six years younger than his brother. They were described as all bright and promising children.

The Alger's home, built in 1885 on Fort Street in Detroit. (Later razed.)

Following his term as governor, Alger didn't seek re-election and the family moved into their new, handsome and huge mansion on Fort Street in Detroit. Some compared it in size to the Fort Shelby Hotel.

Alger was appointed Secretary of War in Washington, D.C., in 1897 by President William McKinley, and held the post until his resignation in August of 1899. Two years later (September 1902) he was appointed to fill and unexpired term in the U.S. Senate and in January 1903, he was elected to a full term by the Michigan Legislature.

The Algers had their own railroad car, "Michigan," for traveling and while in Washington they lived in a beautiful home. Annette became known for her social graces and good taste during these years.[4] They gained a reputation for entertaining with great flair.

Russell A. Alger
State Archives

They had, in fact, planned a farewell party for Alger on February 5, 1907, as his Senate term was expiring on March 4 and he had not sought re-election. The invitations were ready to mail out when he died suddenly, from heart failure, on January 24, 1907.

"The Moorings," the mansion of Russell Alger, Jr. (northern view), where Annette lived at the time of her death. It is now the Grosse Pointe War Memorial, on the shore of Lake St. Clair.

Annette continued carrying out Alger's philanthropic work and lived in downtown Detroit until 1911, when their house was demolished. She moved to Grosse Pointe Farms where her son Russell Alger, Jr. had built an Italian Renaissance style mansion in 1910. Annette died on August 24, 1919, at age 79, and was entombed in the large family mausoleum in Elmwood Cemetery of Detroit.

Russell Jr. died in 1930, and in 1949 the mansion, situated on Lake St. Clair, was deeded to the Grosse Pointe War Memorial Association. ❖

❖ Mary Brown Thompson Luce ❖

Wife of

Governor Cyrus G. Luce

1887 through 1890

ccording to her hometown newspaper at the time of her death, "Mrs. Luce was emphatically a Michigan woman, and a woman whom Michigan delighted to honor."[1]

Thirty-six years earlier, when the *Coldwater Republican* newspaper published an announcement about the marriage of Cyrus Gray Luce to Mrs. Mary E. Thompson on November 8, 1883, it stated, "Mrs. Darwin Thompson is too well known to need an introduction."

To those not living in the small town, this latter report might be mystifying. But a look into Mary's life reveals why she was accorded such affection and respect.

Mary Eliza Brown was born in Cambria of Hillsdale County in 1843. She was the eldest of six children and her mother died when she was not yet 10 years old. The little girl took care of as many of her sisters and brothers that remained together.

When Mary was 16, she married her first husband, Darwin A. Thompson. She gave birth to three children; two sons and a daughter. They all died in childhood. After 22 years of marriage, her husband died in 1881. She then went to live with her younger sister, Mrs. W. H. Wieand, in Bronson. It was here that Mary met Cyrus Luce of nearby Coldwater.

Mary was described as being pert and active, attractive and style conscious, and was 19 years younger than Luce when they married two years later.[2] They began their married life in the farm home where he'd lived 33 years with his first wife.

Luce, born July 2, 1824, was the second of six sons in a pioneering family from Ohio. They had moved to Indiana and he had come to Coldwater in 1848. He married his first wife, Julia A. Dickinson, from Gilead, the next year. The couple homesteaded 80 acres of wild land near Gilead, in Branch County. They had five children before her death in August of 1882 at age 52: Elmira, Emery, Dwight (who died in infancy), Florence, and Homer. Four of them were living when Luce and Mary were married and she was a tender, devoted mother to them.

Luce had been active in local politics since 1852 and was first elected to the state legislature in 1854, subsequently serving in both the House and Senate. In less than three years after their marriage, Luce was elected Governor of Michigan and they moved to Lansing.

"Becoming Michigan's First Lady made no apparent change in this little gentlewoman. Always poised and gracious, she made her way without effort, never at a loss how to act, because following her natural impulses of courtesy gave her peculiar charm and won friends everywhere."[3]

Mary was considered a social favorite during their years in Lansing. Both she and the Governor were members of the U and I Club there and she had many friends throughout the state. She was noted for her patience, self-control, and generosity. She was also said to be quick in discerning right from wrong and firm in following what she felt to be right.

Cyrus and Mary spent the entire summer of 1888 on Mackinac Island and Mary was therefore considered the first hostess at the Summer Executive Mansion on Mackinac Island.[4] Since that time it has been the custom of many governors' families to spend their summers on the island. It was not until 1935, however, that the Mackinac Island State Park Commission set aside one of the houses within the state park for the use of the governor of Michigan. Ten years later the state purchased the present Governor's Summer Residence for this purpose.[5]

During their stay on the island, one of the generals at Fort Mackinac had fallen ill with a sudden chill and was on a cot in a suite of tents, next to governmental headquarters. Mary was found down on her knees by the little camp stove building a fire. When remonstrated with, she said: "He needed the fire and I couldn't find the orderly, so of course I made it,"... a logic which might not have occurred to many in her position.[6]

When the Governor and staff went into camp with the National Guard each year, the boys looked upon Mary almost as a mother. They greeted her carriage with cheers.

Mary accompanied Luce when he headed a Michigan delegation to Pennsylvania to dedicate the Michigan Cavalry Monument on June 18, 1889. The monument marked the field where the cavalry fought during the Battle of Gettysburg.

After his two terms in office, the Governor and Mary moved back to Coldwater where he ran his farm,

Cyrus G. Luce
State Archives

63

tended his business interests, and was active in the Michigan Grange. He died on March 18, 1905, at the age of 80.

Mary lived 15 years longer than Luce and continued her activities in local clubs, including membership of the Presbyterian Ladies Aid. She was a friend and inseparable companion of her stepdaughter, Florence, until her death on January 18, 1920. Mary was buried in Oak Grove Cemetery in Coldwater with other members of the Luce family.

On August 15, 1975, the Governor Cyrus Gray Luce Homesite was listed in the State Register of Historic Sites. By this time, the Public Safety Building was standing on the location, the northeast corner of Division Street and East Washington Street in Coldwater. ❖

Mary with Governor Luce and the Michigan delegation at a June 1889 dedication ceremony in Gettysburg.

❖ Elizabeth G. Winans ❖

Wife of

Governor Edwin B. Winans

1891 and 1892

lizabeth Galloway Winans, described as a courageous woman and devoted to her husband, played a vital role in the life of Governor Edwin Baruch Winans. She married him when her sister wouldn't and influenced him to return to Michigan after they'd moved to California.

Edwin was an only child, born on May 16, 1826, in Avon, New York. At the age of 8, he came with his parents, John and Eliza Way Winans, and settled on a farm near Unadilla, in Livingston County. His father died and he moved with his mother to Pettysville, four miles west of Hamburg. Here he found work in a wool-carding and dyeing establishment, and continued his education as best he could. When he was twenty, he entered Albion College and spent two years preparing for law school, but in 1850 decided to go with two friends to search for gold in California.[1]

Five years later, having opened a bank with a partner in the mining town of Rough and Ready, he was well established. He returned to Hamburg by way of Panama to marry Sarah Galloway, the girl he'd left behind. Sarah, however, wasn't enthusiastic about leaving for California and refused to go.

Courtesy of Duane L. Zemper

"Take Lib," she said, pointing to her sister, Elizabeth, with a laugh. Winans knew Lib as well as Sarah, so he proposed to her at once. She accepted.[2] Elizabeth was nineteen, ten years younger than Winans. They had a very short courtship, but the prospect of adventure obviously appealed to her. They were married on September 3, 1855, and soon left for the West. Their first son, George G., was born in Rough and Ready, and although Elizabeth tolerated life there for three years she wanted to return home. Considering her wishes, Winans sold his business and they sailed for Michigan.

They had to bring their money in gold coins along with them. Winans carried the coins in two stout satchels and wore a Colt's revolver on his hip. Elizabeth, thinking it would help him if she carried some of the weight, had quilted part of the coins into a heavy dress. After one day, however, she discovered it was too heavy for her to carry. When they got to New York, they exchanged the coins for bank credits.[3]

Back home, the couple settled on her family's farm in Hamburg Township, where Elizabeth had been born on January 15, 1836. She was the youngest of George and Susan Haight Galloway's six children. They had come to Michigan while it was still a territory and were among Livingston County's earliest pioneers.[4] Elizabeth and Edwin eventually bought the 400-acre farm from her brother. It became known as the Winans' Farm where she led a quiet family life and remained for the rest of her days.

With Winans, however, it was a different matter. Within two years from the time they'd arrived back at Hamburg, Winans had campaigned and been elected to the State House of Representatives. He served two consecutive terms and remained in public life from then on.

About 1869 the Winans built a new house on the bank overlooking Pleasant Lake, which became known as Winans' Lake. It was here that their second son, Edwin B. Winans, Jr. was born. Their family life was simple and wholesome. Elizabeth was a competent and thrifty housewife. She'd allow no other cook in her kitchen. The table was always bountifully supplied with good things to eat and there was always room and a welcome for a friend or a chance wayfarer.[5]

Winans was elected as probate judge in 1877 and served four years. In 1882 he was elected to the U.S. Congress and re-elected in 1884.

In 1890, Winans was elected the first Democrat Governor in 40 years. Elizabeth was described as "an educated, refined woman, whose mental attainments and social qualities fit her for the position which she occupies as hostess of the Gubernatorial Mansion."[6] The reference to the Gubernatorial Mansion was, of course, the Winans' home.

During the one term he served as governor, Winans continued his practice of going back to the farm whenever he could, and was called the Farmer Governor. He did not seek re-election, returned home, and died a year-and-a-half later on July 4, 1894.

While Winans was pursuing his political career, their sons were growing up and both served in the United States Army. George attained the rank of Major and served as his father's private secretary while he was governor. Edwin graduated from West Point and was a Brigadier General at Fort Oglethorpe, Georgia, at the time of his mother's death.

Edwin B. Winans
State Archives

During his 42 years of service Edwin was in Mexico with General John Pershing and overseas during World War I. Edwin was called Ned, and Elizabeth would say, "As long as Ned is in the United States, I feel he is near home."

A member of the Episcopal Church for 60 years, Elizabeth lived in their home at Winans' Lake for 32 years after her husband's death. She was affectionately called "Grandma Winans" by the neighborhood children. One of these children was the late Mrs. Ferdinand (Minnie) Cox, who recalled that "Grandma Winans was a very gracious woman and not too large a woman.

"She and her sister, Aunt Julie, a maiden lady, lived together in the lovely, very large mansion," Minnie said. "It burned some years ago, was rebuilt, and is now the Lakeland Country Club, three miles north of Hamburg."[7]

Julie died on January 14, and Elizabeth died a few weeks later on February 2, 1926, at the age of 90. She was buried in the Hamburg Cemetery beside her husband. Elizabeth was survived by her sons, three grandchildren, and five great-grandchildren.[8]

A plaque was erected near the Hamburg Cemetery in Governor Winans' honor by the Michigan Historical Commission in 1986. ❖

(Left to Right) Julia Galloway, Elizabeth Winans, and Mrs. Edward Bode on the front porch of the Winans home.   *Howell Area Archives*

❖ Lucretia W. Rich ❖

Wife of

Governor John T. Rich

1893 through 1896

ucretia W. Rich is remembered by those who knew her for the very fancy dresses she wore and is described as having been "a very fine lady who displayed good breeding."[1]

The eighth of nine children, Lucretia was born on February 7, 1836, in Avon of Livingston County, New York, to Samuel and Nancy Lasen Winship. She was about 6 months old when the family made the long, hard trip from New York State to Michigan. They settled in their new home in Atlas Township of Genesee County. During her early school years she attended the country school and later taught in local schools for several years.[2]

What Lucretia lacked in formal education, she more than made up by extensive reading and her interest in the social arts. When she was 26, Lucretia married John T. Rich, a few years her junior. He was the stepson of her eldest sister, Anna. Rich, born April 23, 1841, in Pennsylvania, had come to Elba Township in Lapeer County with his father after his mother died. His father then married Anna Winship.

Lucretia and John T. were married on March 12, 1862. The couple never had children and as his public offices moved from local to state and then national positions. Lucretia spent most of her time traveling with him.

Courtesy (The Ven) Charles D. Braidwood

During their marriage, Rich served as Michigan Legislator in both Houses, a U.S. Congressman, and governor of Michigan. While he was governor, the couple lived in the Hotel Downey of Lansing.

Lucretia was busy in community affairs while he was governing. She was quite prominent in the founding of Sparrow Hospital. It was started by women volunteers and was to provide a hospital for people in state government. The doors were to always be open to the indigent and this policy continues to the present day.[3]

After two terms as governor, Rich did not run for re-election. "At the time Mr.

Rich was Governor, no one had been a candidate for election for more than two terms, and he respected that tradition."[4] He also may have been urged by Lucretia to retire at that time because of threats against him.

Rich had not endeared himself to the politicians in Lansing. Convinced they had certified passage of an amendment increasing the salaries of certain state officers when it had actually been defeated, he promptly gave three of them the boot. The secretary of state, state treasurer and state land commissioner were all removed from office. Rich recalled later:

"There were vague rumors that I was in danger of bodily harm. My wife advised me not to walk alone at night between the State House and our hotel."[5]

After leaving the governorship, Rich was appointed Collector of Customs in Detroit, and later, in Port Huron. Each time, Lucretia lived with him in the city where his work was centered. They spent some weekends on their farm, south of Elba, which had been his father's, but only had an office and a bedroom there. His nephew ran the farm for them and they never had a permanent home of their own. "Just a place to hang their hats."[6]

During the last years of her life, Lucretia was not well and could not travel with Rich as she was accustomed. So she stayed in Elba with her sister, Melissa, and a niece, who lived near the train depot. This made it easier for John T., as he was called, to come and go while taking care of his official business. He was appointed state treasurer in 1908 by Governor Fred Warner to fill a vacancy caused by the involuntary resignation of the treasurer who had been serving.

Another sister, Pamelia, recorded Lucretia's death in her diary. She wrote on May 21, 1912: "Lucretia... left just before sun down... without a struggle." She was buried in Mt. Hope Cemetery of Lapeer. Fourteen years later, Rich was also buried there after dying in St. Petersburg, Florida, on March 28, 1926.

John T. Rich
State Archives

Almost four years after Lucretia's death, Rich married Georgia Winship, who was the daughter of Lucretia's brother, Nehemiah Winship. She was a spinster with a strong will but without financial means and it was a mutual arrangement, common in those days. This led to some rather uncommon situations when the nephews, of whom the Richs' were very fond, had offspring of their own. Sam Painter of Davison, for example, pointed out that his great-grandfather was Lucretia's brother and his mother's father was the brother of Georgia. ❖

The Detroit News

❖ Frances G. Pingree ❖

Wife of

Governor Hazen S. Pingree

1897 through 1900

Despite the fact that Governor Hazen Pingree was considered an outstanding mayor of Detroit and a two-term governor, First Lady Frances Pingree grew so skeptical about politics that she eventually withdrew into seclusion.

Attractive and intelligent, Frances A. Gilbert was a 32 year-old schoolteacher in Mt. Clemens when she and Pingree were married on February 28, 1872.

Pingree, born in Maine on August 30, 1840, had served in the Civil War and spent nearly five months as a prisoner of war in Andersonville. He was mustered out of service in August of 1865 and returned to his home in the East. He came shortly after to Detroit and was employed by H. P. Baldwin's boot and shoe establishment.[1] Baldwin had been state senator and a few years later (1868) was elected governor of Michigan, so Pingree had an early taste of politics.

In 1866, Pingree and a partner purchased a small boot and shoe manufacturing company, forming Pingree and Smith. It became one of three largest manufacturers in the West.

Francis and Pingree were married six years after he'd started his own business and he'd begun building a mansion at 1020 Woodward Avenue a year before their wedding. Their children were born here: Gertrude, in 1874; Hazen Jr., called "Joe," in 1877; and Hazel, in 1880.[2]

The mansion had a stone exterior and the interior was furnished with impressive, extremely expensive French pieces. In the central hall was a tapestry that had belonged to Napoleon Bonaparte. The sitting room was furnished with mahogany chairs covered with satin damask, maroon plush draperies, and a dull ivory maroon table with a circular marble top.

The drawing room contained gilded chairs, rare works of art, crystal chandeliers, and white marble mantles. Pingree's favorite piece was "a table with a carved onyx and brass standard and a circular porcelain top depicting Louis XV surrounded by medallions of court beauties."[3]

Pingree was elected mayor of Detroit in 1889 and immediately started making reforms to help the common man. In doing this he fought against special interests and monopolistic corporations, which led him into conflict with people they'd previously considered friends. As a result, Frances was snubbed socially.[4]

Frances was credited with giving her husband the idea of helping city dwellers during the depression by giving them vacant city land and seed potatoes to plant. The program was soon referred to as "Pingree's potato patches," and he became known as "Potato Patch Pingree."

Hazen S. Pingree
State Archives

71

Although Pingree probably enjoyed the references, Frances may not have appreciated them. Their daughter, Gertrude, died at the age of 19 (March 26, 1893), and Frances began to withdraw from society.

"She (Frances) didn't approve of the use of alcohol, tobacco or profanity... and looked upon politics with a jaundiced eye," her great-grandson, C. Hazen Pingree, pointed out. "Great-grandfather also brought his surviving parent, his father, to live with them. This probably didn't help much."

Frances tried, but obviously had a hard time keeping a rein on her husband. Malcolm Bingay, then managing editor of the *Detroit Free Press*, told of visiting "Ping" in the mid-1890s. He was led downstairs in their home where Pingree pried loose a brick in the basement wall and brought out a flask of whiskey to restore their spirits.

Governor and Frances Pingree raised their family in this mansion on Woodward Avenue. The Rackham Memorial building now stands on the site. Detroit Historical Museum

By the time Pingree was elected governor, "Mrs. Pingree, who had been shocked by the character of her husband's tempestuous career, had withdrawn into seclusion in the Pingree home. Although the First Lady of Michigan, she never accompanied the Governor on any of his official appearances."[5]

After serving two terms, the feisty Governor went elephant hunting in South Africa, visited Germany on his return, and became ill. Friends took him to London, but he died there. His body was brought back to Detroit and he was buried on June 18, 1901.

Frances continued living in their Woodward Avenue home until her death at age 67, on July 21, 1907. A five line obituary in the *Detroit News* on July 22 noted the burial was private and stated, "Please omit flowers." Her body was placed beside her husband in their private mausoleum in Woodlawn Cemetery, Detroit.

Frances was survived by their daughter, Hazel Pingree Depew, who had two daughters before her second marriage to Wilson W. Mills. Hazel lived in Grosse Pointe until her death in 1976.

The Pingree's son, Joe, and his wife, Alice, had a son named Gilbert, for his grand-mother's maiden name. Gilbert married, and his widow, Katharine, lives in his home in Grosse Pointe today. Gilbert's son, C. Hazen Pingree, lives in Fort Wayne, Indiana.

The Pingree mansion, across the side street from the Detroit Institute of Arts, was razed and this is now the site of the Horace H. Rackham Educational Memorial Building. Despite the Governor's on-going battle with industrialists, he was a champion of the common people and "...the first to awake to the great inequalities in taxation and to initiate steps for reform." A statue was erected in his honor in Detroit's West Grand Circus Park, memorializing him as "Idol of the People."[6] ❖

❖ Allaseba P. Bliss ❖

Wife of

Governor Aaron T. Bliss

1901 through 1904

Governor Aaron Bliss and his wife, Allaseba, had known each other since their early childhood days in New York. From the time of their marriage they united their efforts to become successful in business and government.

Allaseba Morey Phelps was born on November 7, 1835, in Solsville, located in Madison County, New York. She was the daughter of a prosperous farmer, Ambrose Phelps.[1]

Bliss, also from Madison County, was born on May 22, 1837, and raised on his family farm. He entered the service as a private and rose to the rank of Captain during the Civil War. Following his discharge in 1865, Bliss moved to Saginaw and started logging. After a year or so, he formed a lumber company with his brother, Dr. Lyman W. Bliss and J. H. Jerome (Jerome's daughter, Mary, married Dr. Bliss and the two families claimed two Michigan governorships within the next 20 years).

When his business ventures were doing well and expanding, Bliss returned to New York to marry Allaseba on March 31, 1868. They came to Zilwaukee immediately after the wedding, where the Bliss Brothers' Mill was located. Allaseba assisted the growing company by overseeing the boarding house where the mill workers lived.

Historical Society of Saginaw County

In later years, Allaseba recalled their house in Zilwaukee. It was one of only three rooms and during the first warm season the mosquito pest was awesome. She could not finish her household duties in the evening without being protected by a smudge pan which her brother-in-law held near where she was working.[2]

After two years in Zilwaukee the couple moved to Saginaw, and by 1873 they were financially able to build a mansion on North Michigan Avenue. Beautiful woods were used in its construction. The floors were of elaborate inlaid patterns, huge mirrors in frames of walnut and mahogany adorned the walls… all representative of the lumber which had brought them their fortune.

Elaborate parties were given, with crinoline-gowned women coming down the mahogany grand staircase to meet their escorts and be greeted by their gracious hostess, Allaseba.[3]

Bliss was elected to the state senate in 1882 and Russell Alger, another lumber baron, was elected governor in 1885. Alger appointed Bliss as a member of his staff with the rank of Colonel.[4]

In 1888, Bliss was elected to the U.S. Congress and Allaseba accompanied him to Washington, D.C. "She enjoyed the opportunities that two years of life in the capital afford to wives of prominent congressmen."[5] Upon their return to Michigan, Colonel Bliss campaigned for the governorship, was elected, and took office in January of 1901.

During the next four years, Allaseba met the responsibilities and enjoyed the privileges that come to a First Lady. She was referred to as "mistress of the Executive Mansion," the mansion being their own home in Saginaw.

Allaseba was extremely active in many local charitable, cultural, and religious institutions. She contributed generously to building of the Methodist Church and served on its official board for many years. She was a lifelong member of the Daughters of the American Revolution. She was one of the founders, and for many years a member of the Board of Directors of Saginaw General Hospital. She was also state president and national officer of the Woman's Relief Corps.

Governor John T. Rich named Allaseba to the board of the Industrial School for Girls in Adrian. She was the only woman to hold an appointive office during his administration and she continued to serve for a total of eight years.

Bliss died less that two years after his two terms as governor, on September 16, 1906, while seeking treatment in a Milwaukee sanatorium for a heart condition. Allaseba, however, continued to be active during the next 12 years. She traveled extensively, visiting nearly all of the capitals in Europe, and spent her winters in Florida or California.[6]

Allaseba observed her 80th birthday by holding an open house for her many friends. Three years later she died, on July 17, 1918, after an illness of several weeks. The couple had no children, and in the year following her death, the Bliss residential show place was sold from their estate and converted into 14 apartments.

Both Allaseba and Aaron Bliss were buried in the Forest Lawn Cemetery of Saginaw. ❖

Aaron Bliss
State Archives

❖ Martha D. Warner ❖

Wife of

Governor Fred M. Warner

1905 through 1910

 usan Edessa Slocum described her mother and father, Martha and Governor Fred M. Warner: "They were both plain people, nothing 'put-on' about them."[1]

Both Warners were exceptional, however, in many ways. Martha entertained politicians and indirectly helped Warner in his rise to the governorship. She also was at his side in some of the state affairs in Lansing. He was the first Michigan Governor to serve three consecutive terms.

Martha M. Davis was born in 1866, the daughter of Samuel and Susan Graft Davis in Farmington Township, Oakland County. Her parents owned a large farm near Farmington. Fred, having been adopted as a 7 month-old baby in 1886, was raised in the largest, most imposing home in the small village of Farmington. The two would have known each other.

Fred had gone to Michigan Agricultural College and left after one term, returning to work in his father's general merchandising store. He was a highly eligible bachelor and Martha was an attractive girl. They were married on September 19, 1888.

A year after their marriage Warner established a cheese factory in Farmington. By 1906, there were more than a dozen other highly successful cheese factories. In 1915, the Fred M. Warner Cheese Company became the Warner Dairy Company.

During these years, Martha gave birth to five children. An infant, born in 1890, did not survive. Susan Edessa was born in 1891, Howard Maltby was born in 1893, Harley Davis was born in 1894, and Helen Rhoda was born in 1899. After the birth of Susan Edessa, called Edessa, the family moved into the elder Warner's big house which later became known as the "Governor's Mansion."

While the family and the cheese businesses were growing, Warner was climbing the political ladder, from village president to state senator, 1894 to 1898; secretary of state, 1900 to 1904; and on to governor in 1904. Martha entertained guests and the children helped with a few antics of their own. On one occasion she served a chicken dinner on the lawn of their home to more than 60 members of the Republican Newspaper Association of Michigan.[2]

Following the Governor's swearing-in ceremonies, a festive reception was held in the Capitol Building with the Governor and Martha heading the reception line. The band played in the Rotunda, there was dancing in the corridors, and refreshments were served in the offices of the Department of State.

"Mother went with Father part time to Lansing," Edessa recalled. "Then the family rented a house and moved up there for a few months.

"Mother was a wonderful person, a plain, every day person. She didn't particularly like social events, in my opinion." Edessa continued, "At home she did every everything except run the dairy.

"She was a large woman, with dark hair and a happy disposition. I can't remember my mother ever being cross," Edessa said. "She was nice to everyone. She always wanted to help others."

Warner took the oath of office for his second term in his bed at their home. He had been ill and was too weak to travel to Lansing for the ceremony. "He said 'I do' to the oath, affirmed his signature to the document, (said a few words)... and kissed his little daughter, Helen." Martha invited the few people present to stay for lunch.[3]

In May of 1907, President Theodore Roosevelt came to Lansing for the 50th Anniversary of the Michigan Agricultural College (MAC). Martha was not in the three mile parade from the Capitol to the college, but she was a guest at the luncheon held at the home of the MAC president.

Martha and their four children were present in Lansing for Warner's third swearing-in as governor. His oath of office was administered by Chief Justice of the Supreme Court, Charles Blair, the son of former Governor Austin Blair.

After the governorship, having spent 16 years in state politics, Warner could spend more time with his family in Farmington. He returned to farming, banking and real estate interests. With the children in school, Martha devoted time to community affairs, the Farmington Chapter of the Eastern Star, the Village Guild to improve the village, the Cemetery Association, and the Methodist Church.

Fred Warner
State Archives

The Warners had gone to Florida after the first of the year in 1923, but he had been suffering for some time with uremic poisoning and died April 17 in a sanatorium in Orlando. He was 57 years old. Martha continued to maintain their home in Farmington until her death in 1949.

Their son, Harley, died in an auto accident in 1931; Howard died in 1958; Helen married Clair Gaukler and lived in Pontiac, until her death in 1979; Edessa married William Slocum and they lived in the family mansion, until her death in 1980. Their children, Susan Slocum Klingbeil and William Slocum, gave the Governor's Mansion to the city of Farmington in 1980, and it is now the Farmington Historical Museum. ❖

The Warner Mansion, 33805 Grand River Avenue in Farmington, is now the home of Farmington Historical Museum.   *Farmington Historical Museum*

❖ Lillian J. Osborn ❖

Wife of

Governor Chase S. Osborn

1911 and 1912

 illian Osborn deserved an accolade of her own for having kept up with Governor Chase Osborn as long as she did. He was one of Michigan's most flamboyant, extravagant, energetic and unconventional governors. She married him when she was 18 years old and was First Lady during the years he was governor.

"I had the time of my life," 81 year-old Osborn recalled his two gubernatorial years.[1] Lillian probably wouldn't have applied the same description to her life at the time. A serene person, she took an active role in many phases of her husband's strenuous career, but her chief role was caring for their growing family.

Born on May 5, 1863, Lillian Gertrude Jones was raised in Milwaukee, Wisconsin. A pretty young girl, she met Chase Salmon Osborn when he was a 21 year-old reporter on the local newspaper. He was an Indiana native and courted her for some time before they were married on May 7, 1881. He was earning $12 a week and her wedding bouquet on that Saturday night was a five-cent one he'd bought at the German market.

State Archives

"Our wedding trip was on a streetcar... five cents apiece. In fact, we had passes," Osborn later recalled.[2] The couple started housekeeping in one room with part-time use of a cooking stove. The first of their seven children, Ethel Lenore, was born here in 1882. A year later, Osborn bought the *Mining News*, in Florence, Wisconsin, on the Michigan border. They had $80 when they left for Florence and two more children were born while they lived there. George Augustus was born in 1884 and Lillian Marguerite was born in 1886.[3]

The paper became profitable and when Osborn sold it in 1887, he had nearly $10,000 with which he bought the *Evening News* in Sault Ste. Marie, Michigan. The growing family moved to the Upper Peninsula, making it their permanent home.

While he was running the paper, Osborn was appointed to several state government positions and became so interested in politics that he made an unsuccessful bid for a congressional seat in 1896.

Lillian, meanwhile, had not been having an easy time. Their fourth child, Chase Salmon Jr., was born in January of 1888. A fifth child, Emily Fisher, was born in November of 1889. Their 4 year-old daughter, Lillian, died only a few months later in February of 1890. A sixth child, Oren Chandler, was born in December of 1891 and died when less than 9 months old, the following September.

While Osborn was juggling his newspaper work and a blossoming political career, Lillian was raising, birthing, and burying their children. Their seventh child, Miriam Gertrude was born on April 17, 1900. Osborn made a run for governor that fall but was defeated.

Little Miriam died less than two months after her second birthday, on June 14, 1902. Lillian survived the heartbreaks with a strength of character that carried her through the years to come.

Although the Osborns lived in a small house at first, they built a larger and grander one in Sault Ste. Marie. They also built a summer camp on Duck Island, where three log houses were named Big Duck, Little Duck, and The Gander.

"Duck Island is a small Island in the St. Mary's River, adjacent to Sugar Island. The Gander was the largest of the three log houses and actually is located on Sugar, rather than Duck Island," according to their granddaughter, Ann Osborn Pratt. "The Governor's large collection of books and memorabilia of his active life was kept in the 'Go-Down'… a cement block, sizable building between Big and Little Ducks."[4] The Duck Island property is now owned by the University of Michigan.

After Osborn was defeated in his 1900 bid for governor, he devoted his time to business matters. His investments in timber lands and discovery of a vast iron range in Ontario, Canada, made him wealthy. He could afford to re-enter politics. In 1908, he was appointed regent of the University of Michigan by Governor Fred Warner, and in 1910 he was elected governor of Michigan.

"While Osborn was in Lansing he owned a house there, I've been told, which he purchased for his eldest daughter, Ethel, and her husband, Adam E. Ferguson," according to their granddaughter. "It's been my under-standing that Lillian never moved to Lansing, but visited there and reportedly entertained guests with the Governor. She was active in literary clubs at the Soo, had a large circle of friends, and was greatly loved in the community."

Osborn liked to travel and, after his stint as governor, Lillian went to Africa with him. He left her, the only white woman at their camp, for a period of time while he ventured farther into the jungle. Fortunately, Lillian had stamina, courage, and was an outdoor person. She was able to cope under the stress of unusual circumstances.

Chase S. Osborn
State Archives

She also possessed a delightful sense of humor which was a saving grace on many occasions."[5]

Osborn, who seemed to make money on everything he touched, decided early to keep only what he needed for a living and to give the rest away. An excellent rider, he had a fine string of horses until he decided it was healthier to walk. He gave them all away. He donated thousands of acres of land to various individuals, universities, and along with other donations, managed to dispense his great wealth by 1940.

"As far as I know, Grandmother never questioned the giving away of money... and they lived well," her granddaughter said. "She was an extremely patient, gentle person and a gracious hostess. A marvelous mother and grandmother, she genuinely enjoyed life."

In later years the Osborns were separated. She died on February 4, 1948 and was buried in Riverside Cemetery of Sault Ste. Marie with their three children who had pre-deceased her. Osborn died a year later, April 11, 1949, and was buried on his beloved Duck Island.

They were survived by four of their children: Ethel, who died in 1976; George, who died in 1972 (the father of Ann Osborn Pratt); Chase S. Jr., who moved to Santa Cruz, California, and died there in 1982; and Emily, who married Richard Sanderson and lived in Sun City, Arizona, at the time of her death in 1979. As of September 1992, Lillian and Chase Osborn were survived by five of their 12 grandchildren, and 22 great grandchildren. ❖

❖ Historical Note

Researching records is complicated because Stellanova or Stella Brunt Osborn is listed in various relationships. According to *Michigan Today,* a University of Michigan publication, dated June 1986, in Vol. 18, No.2, page 4: She (Stella) was a student at the University of Michigan when Osborn was a regent and wrote to thank him for sponsoring Robert Frost as the U-M's Poet-in-Residence for ten months on campus, 1921 to 1922. They corresponded and he adopted her in 1931 as his secretary, collaborator, and daughter. She was 34 years his junior. The adoption was dissolved, however, and they married in April of 1949 after the death of his first wife. Two days later, he died at the age of 89.

Ferris State University Archives

❖ Helen G. Ferris ❖

Wife of

Governor Woodbridge N. Ferris

1913 through 1916

Although Helen Ferris suffered from a long illness and remained in Big Rapids while her husband, Woodbridge Nathan Ferris, served two terms as governor, she had a great influence on him. He wrote a daily letter to her while he was at the capital and "made her familiar with the important problems of the state."

"I always shielded her so far as possible, from the thousand and one petty annoyances that came to me in my public life," Ferris recalled after her death. "For the best service I rendered Michigan, Mrs. Ferris deserves a large part of the merited commendation. Her sense of justice, her purity of motive, her Christian democracy illumined my pathway."[1]

Helen or "Nellie" as Ferris always called her, taught at his side for 20 years and helped him found Ferris Industrial School in Big Rapids. Ferris Industrial School started with only two small rooms and 15 students. Helen was his sole assistant. The school grew to become Ferris Institute and eventually became Ferris State University.[2]

Helen Frances was born to John C. and Martha House Gillespie in New Haven, New York. She was born on September 7, 1853. Helen was the fourth of their five children. When she was approximately 13 years old, she attended a private girls school.

A classmate described Helen as being slightly taller than the other girls in their room. "She had very beautiful, long blonde hair which she wore parted in the middle and waved on either side and neatly coiled in the back. Never a hair was misplaced... She had a fresh, clear complexion and very expressive eyes."[3]

After teaching two terms in a country school, Helen entered the Oswego Normal and Training School in Oswego, New York, to obtain her teacher's certificate. She was only 16 years old at the time. A year later, Ferris enrolled at the Oswego Normal and Training School and fell in love with her. They became engaged, but she left to teach a year in the public schools of Franklin, Indiana. That fall she returned to New York and the couple was married on December 23, 1874.

Five days after their marriage, Helen began teaching with him in the Spencer Academy in Spencer, New York. A year later, in 1875, they moved to Freeport, Illinois, to organize a business college and academy. In the spring of 1876, they moved again. This time to Dixon, Illinois, where Ferris was in charge of the Normal Department of the Rock River University.

Helen taught almost continuously during this period. Their first son, Carlton Gillespie, was born on September 18, 1876, in the university dormitory. They moved next to Pittsfield, Illinois, where they lived for five years. Their second son, Clifford Wendell, was born there on June 3, 1881. He died on September 20, 1881. He was a victim of what was then called cholera infantum.

In the summer of 1884, the young family moved to Big Rapids and founded Ferris Industrial School. Their third son, Phelps Fitch, was born on April 16, 1889. From the very beginning of Ferris Industrial School's history, Helen taught regular classes and did her own housework; but, by 1901 her health failed and she had to give up her classroom work.

Despite this, Helen still maintained her interest in the students and kept open house for them. She read aloud for an hour to as many as 16 boys every Sunday night during the long, cold winter months. "Hundreds of students have precious memories of her inspiring instruction and self-sacrifice."[4]

1913

Although Ferris claimed he had no political ambition, he ran for Congress in 1892, but was an unsuccessful candidate. Ferris also made a losing bid for the governorship in 1904. Helen was keenly sensitive to unkind criticism and when her husband was urged to again become a gubernatorial candidate in 1912, she let it be known that there wasn't much point in it. When he decided to run, however, she became his most enthusiastic helper. And, as Ferris later wrote, "Naturally she was elated over my final success."[5]

Helen loved great books, especially American biographies. She "avoided novels that discussed sex problems," Ferris recalled. "She loved beautiful surroundings, beautiful flowers, beautiful books, beautiful trees, and beautiful human characters." She also possessed a keen sense of humor. Helen belonged to only a few social and public associations. Speaking to any audience was impossible for her, however, due to her inborn timidity.[6]

Woodbridge N. Ferris
State Archives

84

Helen Ferris died on March 23, 1917, less than three months after her husband left the Office of Governor. Her body was placed in the family Mausoleum in the Big Rapids Cemetery.

Ferris married his second wife, Mary Ethel McLoud from Indianapolis, Indiana, on August 14, 1921. He was elected a U.S. Senator in 1922, a post he held until his death in 1929. ❖

Courtesy of Dr. Clark Herrington

❖ Mary M. Sleeper ❖

Wife of

Governor Albert E. Sleeper

1917 through 1920

Mary Sleeper was a confident, calm person who took things in her stride... including the election of her husband as governor of Michigan.

On August 31, 1916, she wrote in her diary: "Bert Sleeper is nominated for governor. Think of it. What will the harvest be?" Then, on November 7, 1916, she wrote: "A beautiful day. Election day. Bert Sleeper was elected Governor of Michigan. Think of that." The governor-elect caught the train in Bad Axe and left for Detroit that afternoon. In the evening Mary entertained 18 women at their home for bridge. It was her turn to entertain the 500 Club and life obviously went on as usual.

In 1916, most traveling was done by train. If the train was more than five hours late, Mary Sleeper simply went shopping or rented a hotel room and rested. Life was different in those days and yet similarities are revealed in Mary Sleeper's diaries. She wrote one small page daily in a black, leather bound diary, from the time she was 17 years old until her last days.

Mary Charlotte Moore was born in 1862 in Lexington, near Port Huron. Her mother was Sophia Hodges of New Hampshire and her father was Charles H. Moore, also from New Hampshire and Vermont. He'd come to Lexington in 1851 and was a farmer, merchant, and the agent for Woods and Company, a lumbering company of Cleveland, Ohio. They had three children: Mary, Ella, and Emma.

Albert (Bert) E. Sleeper, born in Vermont on December 31, 1862, had come to Lexington in the fall of 1884. He started in "mercantile pursuits" and as a traveling salesman, but within a few years had established himself in the banking and real estate business. He was president of banks in Yale, Bad Axe, Marlette, Ubly, and of a wholesale gocery company in Bad Axe.

He was elected to the state senate and after completing the first session in 1901, he and Mary were married on July 30, 1901. He was re-elected to another senate term then elected two terms as state treasurer, before being elected governor.[1]

When they were first married, the Sleepers lived in Lexington, but moved to Bad Axe soon after.[2] During all his years in government, Bert had commuted by train to Lansing (later, Stevens drove him at times). Meanwhile, Mary led a fairly serene, well organized life. She ran their household, made and received calls from friends, regularly attended the Episcopal Church, and had an avid interest in libraries. She enjoyed gardening, loved to play bridge, and go to motion pictures and plays.

Mary had no reason to think her life would change. But 1917 entered with her husband's inauguration in Lansing and in less than four months, World War I had begun. Demands on their time became greater for both of them.

Albert E. Sleeper
State Archives

Although the Sleepers had no children of their own, they were very attached to four children of a deceased friend: Phebe, Frances, Stevens, and Helen Clark. Phebe and Stevens lived with them for many years. Mary left her diaries to Phebe's son, Clark Herrington, M.D., who lives in Bad Axe.[3]

"My grandfather and the Governor were close friends in Vermont before he moved to Michigan," Dr. Herrington recalls. "My grandfather came to visit Sleeper and he died while here. He was only 44 years old and he had four children. So, the Governor had the kids, my mother was one of them, come and live with them in the summers." This accounts for the fact that Sleeper liked to be called "Uncle Bert," even when he was governor.

Mary Sleeper stands behind her husband (first woman in the row) watching him sign the Women's Suffrage Bill into law, May 8, 1917, granting women the right to vote for Presidential electors. "Saw Governor Sleeper sign the Suffrage Bill. Surrounded by women," she noted the event later in her diary. State Archives

"My mother, Phebe May Clark, and Mrs. Sleeper were always very close," Herrington said. "Mamie Sleeper was the same as a grandmother to me. When she died, she left her diaries to me, to read."

From her diaries we learn that the Sleepers were building a new house when he was elected governor. "Such a busy time, with building, the congratulating letters, telegrams, and phone calls," she wrote.

November 23, 1916: "Governor (Woodbridge) Ferris here with Bert for dinner. I had to leave early to go visit the hospital." They moved into their new house on December 26 and Mary began packing their trunks for the train ride to Lansing on December 30 for the inauguration. The evening after they arrived, they met many people.

"Such a lot from every place in the state," she wrote.

January 1, 1917: "A great day. A. E. Sleeper made governor of Michigan 12:00 p.m., amidst a large crowd of his nearest and dearest friends. At 8:00 p.m. a reception was held in the Capitol. We stood in line two hours and shook hands."

Three days later Mary "went up to the Capitol and heard Ex-Governor Ferris give his speech and Governor Sleeper, his. Very good indeed." On January 5, she was guest of honor at an afternoon bridge party and the *Mt. Clemens Leader* reported later that Mrs. Sleeper had appeared in Lansing society for the first time. She also made two visits to the state library before returning home to Bad Axe.

April 6, 1917: "WAR DECLARED."

During the next weeks and months, Mary organized a Red Cross Chapter in Huron County, raised funds for the Red Cross, funds for Belgium Babies, and went with Bert to see the boys drilling at MAC (Michigan Agriculture College). She accompanied the Governor to the newly built Camp Custer, near Battle Creek. Drafted men arrived there in September from Michigan and Wisconsin. She attended many patriotic meetings and knit six sweaters for soldiers by the end of the year... many of them while riding on the train.

May 8, 1917: "Went up to the Capitol and saw Governor Sleeper sign the Suffrage bill. Surrounded by women."

By July, Mary was making frequent trips to Lansing. She sat on the platform and made a few remarks at a meeting of the Woman's Preparedness Board. She also worked in a visit "to see Mrs. Spencer at the state library."

Highlights in 1918 included Sleeper's re-election on November 5, and she wrote, "the Influenza is awful bad in the central part of the state. Everything closed up."

November 11, 1918: "THE GREATEST DAY IN THE WORLD, PEACE IS DECLARED. Up at six to see 46 boys off, but they returned at night. A big glorious day."

Mary barely mentioned the many things she did to help other people. She visited the sick, took them for medical treatment and often paid their bills. The latter is revealed only in the financial records she kept at the back of her diary. She gave financial help to libraries, too. She established the Bad Axe Library and helped found the Moore Public Library in Lexington, named for her father .

After Governor Sleeper left office in 1921, he returned to his business interests in Bad Axe.[4] Like other bankers, when the banking holiday was declared in 1933, he suffered great losses. He died on May 13, 1934.

Mary used her own money to pay off the debts after the banks closed. She lived to be 91 years old before she died on October 11, 1953. Both Sleepers were buried in the Lexington Cemetery. Their beautiful home in Bad Axe is now a funeral home.[5] It can be said of Mary Sleeper that, even in her most private diary, she never spoke ill of anyone. ❖

Courtesy of Helen N. Tyrell

❖ Helen K. Green ❖

Wife of

Governor Fred W. Green

1927 through 1930

During Helen Kelly Green's life she experienced a rise to riches and became Michigan's First Lady. It appeared that she had it all. Then her husband died, their daughter was a disappointment to her, and she had to battle to save the family business. An extraordinary woman, she enjoyed the good times and managed to cope well with the difficult ones.

Helen Adelaide Kelly was born in 1875, to William and Adelaide Kelly of Cadillac. After graduating from high school there, she entered the University of Michigan and obtained her teaching degree. She then returned to her hometown and taught high school French for two years before marrying Green.

Fred W. Green was born in Manistee on October 20, 1872, but his family moved to Cadillac when he was young and he and Helen knew each other in high school. Later, while both were students at the university, they dated and began making plans for their future together.[1]

Green began practicing law in Ypsilanti in 1899, served as city attorney of Ypsilanti and became a partner in the Ypsilanti Reed Furniture Company. The couple was married on June 18, 1901, and within three years Green had bought out his business associates and moved the company to Ionia.[2] It became the world's largest manufacturer of rattan furniture. They had their own rattan plantations in the Malay States and had a branch office in Chicago.[3]

During this time, their daughter, Helen Nancy or "Peggy," was born and Helen didn't take an active role in the business, but served as a sounding board.[4] The couple built a Mediterranean style villa in 1924, a mansion with seven bathrooms. In the basement was a large den, constructed to resemble the inside of a log cabin with a huge stone fireplace at one end and Green's hunting trophies on the walls. They were both lovers of oriental art and had a beautiful porcelain Buddha in the basement of their home. They had other rare oriental objects and paintings throughout the house.[5]

Helen had beautiful gardens. She had a rose garden planted by Edgar Guest, who was a friend of theirs. "He brought the roses and planted them," her granddaughter said. On one hand, Helen enjoyed playing bridge with Ionia women and, on the other hand, she was keenly interested in the international peace movement. She corresponded with Stellanova Osborn for many years regarding the organization which was the precursor of the North Atlantic Treaty Organization. The Osborns and the Greens were good friends.

In 1926, Green was elected governor. Ionia was close enough to Lansing, so he was driven back and forth to Lansing, and their home served as a meeting place for political confidants.

Fred W. Green
State Archives

Helen didn't go to the capital very often but she took her First Lady responsibilities seriously and did her part in public events. "She wrote her own speeches and had a great sense of humor," her granddaughter said. "She was unpretentious and always felt inadequate as the Governor's wife."

The Green's daughter, Peggy, eloped, but the marriage didn't work out and she left her 2 year-old child, Helen Tyrrell, with them in 1928. Peggy eloped again and had a second child, Fred Bradley, in this marriage. "My mother married three times (before her death) and each time I would go back to Grandpa and Grandma's," Helen Tyrrell said.[6]

A palatial home for Governor Fred and Helen Green is on a wooded Ionia hilltop, overlooking the Grand River Valley. It was sold to private owners. State Archives

"Grandpa raised Saddlebreds but Grandma didn't ride. Sometimes she might get in a sleigh, but that was all," their granddaughter recalled. "He got me a pony when I was 5 years old, starting me out as a horse woman." She became expert in the art of Dressage and has continued this interest through her life.

Some of her happy childhood memories include time spent at her grandparent's cottage on Long Lake, near Ionia. "It was a hideaway for them," she said.

"One time Grandpa was in a hurry and tossed a pair of trousers to Grandma that needed a button sewed on them. She sewed it on and then sewed a great big one on top of it," granddaughter Helen recalled. "He wore it that way and showed reporters. It made quite a story. Grandma said it was his revenge."

The Greens didn't spend much time on Mackinac Island, although Helen was hostess there in the summer of 1929 for the first National Governor's Conference held in Michigan. (It wasn't until 1935 that the Mackinac Island State Park Commission first set aside one of the houses within the state park for use by the governor of Michigan.)

Green was an avid outdoorsman and was at his lodge near Munising in the Upper Peninsula when he died of peritonitis on November 30, 1936. Their furniture business was in serious financial trouble at the time.

Helen had no alternative but to take over as manager to keep the business going and she did. When matters became critical, she climbed into the family Lincoln, drove to the Ford Motor Company in Dearborn, and talked to Harry Bennett. There had been a long friendship between Bennett and Green from the days when he was governor. Bennett was very close to Henry Ford and he took action. Helen came away with a much needed contract.[7]

Discovering she had an aptitude for business, Helen kept at it until she sold the company and retired in 1947 when she was 73. After being confined to her home for six years by illness, Helen Green died of cancer on November 16, 1957, and was entombed in the Mausoleum in Ionia Cemetery beside her husband.

During the last years of illness, her granddaughter was with Helen and later married her (Helen's) physician, Joseph Foust, M.D., who had five children. The couple had three children of their own, adopted one, and moved to Sacramento, California, in 1970.

Fred was raised by his mother, and joined the U.S. Navy. He continued to make Michigan his home and was the father of five children.

In her will, Helen left her daughter, Peggy, $5,000 in cash, and the residue of the estate to her two grandchildren, Helen Tyrrell and Fred G. Bradley, then a U.S. Navy Lieutenant stationed in Japan. The estate was estimated at $500,000 or more at the time, according to an *Associated Press* report, and the will was contested a month after her death by her daughter.

At Greenview Point, a scenic promontory on the Grand River, just east of Lyons in Ionia County, a memorial to former Governor Green was dedicated on May 29, 1938. A bronze tablet inscription was unveiled on the ten to 16 ton boulder by the Green's 9 year-old granddaughter.

Gerald R. Ford, while minority leader in the U.S. House of Representatives, made the formal dedication of a Michigan Historical Marker in front of the former Green residence at 320 Union Street, in 1973. ❖

❖ Historical Note

Alexander J. Groesbeck, governor for three terms, from 1921 through 1926, was a bachelor, so there was no First Lady during this time.

❖ Clara H. Brucker ❖

Wife of

Governor Wilber Brucker

1931 and 1932

lara Brucker was in her element as First Lady. She had an inquiring mind and a zest for life. During her years in Lansing she was a popular speaker at local club meetings and completed work on her master's degree in political science at Michigan State University.

Described as inimitable and indomitable, she was born in Iowa, one of eight children in the family of the Reverend and Mrs. Emil Hantel. They moved to Saginaw when she was 4 years old.

Clara met Wilber M. Brucker, a Saginaw native and a University of Michigan law student, in 1915. After graduating, he served in the Michigan National Guard and the U.S. Army during World War I. He then returned to practice law in Saginaw where she lived.

Although Brucker wanted to marry Clara Hantel right away, she insisted on finishing her education and getting some experience in the working world.[1] She studied at Drexel Institute in Philadelphia, Pennsylvania, and took courses in journalism at Columbia University. She also worked as a statistician before returning to Michigan and marrying Brucker on August 18, 1923.

"I think I was the first Michigan wife to campaign for her husband," she recalled, referring to his gubernatorial race in 1930. Following his inauguration they rented a three-bedroom house in East Lansing for $50 a month.[2]

Although she considered her husband's wish as her wish, the "charming woman of the gay blue eyes and golden hair" maintained her individuality and was encouraged to do so by Brucker.[3] When Vice President of the United States, Charles Curtis, visited Michigan they had to rely on an affluent resident to entertain him. Clara immediately began a personal but unsuccessful campaign to have the state provide an official residence for governors.

The Bruckers did, however, establish the first Governor's Residence, of sorts, on Mackinac Island, by spending some time in the old Fort in 1931. Rooms were repaired in the former surgeons quarters by the Mackinac Island State Park Commission and Clara spent a month there in the summer with their 4 year-old son, Wilber Jr.

Following his two years as governor, the Bruckers moved to Detroit and Clara was active in many organizations. These included the Salvation Army Auxiliary, Civic Pride Association of Detroit, Women's City Club of Detroit, and the National Institute of the YMCA. She served for 38 years on the Children's Aid Society Board in Detroit.

In 1940, Clara founded the School of Government, a nonpartisan group affiliated with the Federation of Women's Clubs of Detroit, to study government and disseminate information. Clara was the first president of the group and was an active member until the time of her death.

Always busy, one of Clara's favorite hobbies was music. She studied piano, harp, and voice for many years. She took great pride in her collection of antique furniture and Meissen china and was an ardent gardener and loved to swim.

Clara accompanied Brucker to Washington, D.C. in 1954 when he was named General Counsel for Department of Defense. She traveled throughout the world with him when he was appointed Secretary of the Army from July 1955 to January 1961. A journalist by training, she took her camera wherever they went and sometimes this caused her problems. "The White House, the Pentagon, and Buckingham Palace are off-limits to me," she complained. But she built up a collection of more than 4,000 photographs of world officialdom and scenes.[4]

She later used her diaries and photographs taken during this time to write a book, *To Have Your Cake and Eat It,* published in 1968 by Vantage Press.

She said the title of her book summed up her lifetime. "I had felt reservations about marriage in 1923, because I wanted to go abroad and have a career and to me, being a wife meant staying home," she said. "But in writing my book, I suddenly realized that I had managed everything after all."

After Brucker's death at the age of 74, in 1968, Clara continued to maintain their family home in Grosse Pointe Farms and her interest in community activities. "I am very much involved in many civic affairs in Detroit, one of which is Morality in Media," she wrote.[5]

Clara traveled around the world, made trips to Africa, South America, Australia, Russia, and the Scandinavian

Wilber Brucker
State Archives

countries. She took colored slides on all these trips and showed them to groups after she returned.

Close to her heart was her husband's memorabilia, which she sorted to be housed in the Wilber M. Brucker Hall at the United States Army Band Training Center in Fort Myers, Virginia, named in his honor. When the time came for the dedication of the building on March 25, 1978, Clara was on the program, and the portrait she'd commissioned of her husband was unveiled. Following the ceremony, she entertained a large number of dinner guests, which included: her son and daughter-in-law, Mr. and Mrs. Wilber Brucker, Jr.; grandsons Wilbur III and Paul; and granddaughter, Barbara, and her husband, Steven Triggs.[6]

Four months before her death, Clara learned she had leukemia. Always a maverick and an individualist, she would never tell her age. A few days before her death she admitted to being "at least 65." When she died on March 24, 1988, her daughter-in-law, Doris Brucker, said, "Most people would be shocked to think she was 87."[7]

Clara Brucker was buried beside her husband in Arlington National Cemetery in Arlington, Virginia. ❖

❖ Mary Josephine W. Comstock ❖

Wife of

Governor William A. Comstock

1933 and 1934

he Comstocks lived in Ann Arbor during her years as First Lady because tiny Mary Josephine, known as Josephine, didn't care for Lansing and wouldn't move there. Governor William Comstock had a driver who drove him back and forth to the capital.

Her feelings may be understandable, considering the fact that her husband had made three losing campaigns for the governorship before finally being elected. And, once in office, he was faced with intra-party feuding. "Democrats, who for so long had been shut out of patronage, squabbled among themselves over jobs."[1] Party members, in fact, did not nominate Comstock for re-election.

Nonetheless, Josephine entertained a great deal in Ann Arbor. "She did it as a part of her job, but really didn't like people much," her daughter-in-law, Maryanne (Mrs. William Comstock III), recalled.[2]

This, too, is understandable. After their marriage, Comstock began pouring his wealth into an effort to rebuild the Democratic party in Michigan. According to William Muller in a June 17, 1949, *Detroit News* account, "In 1924, the party found itself $37,000 in debt, all of it loaned by Mr. Comstock (A *Detroit Free Press* report claimed that Comstock later tore up the notes). More than once Mr. Comstock under-wrote the expenses of the Michigan delegation to Democratic national conventions," ...Muller continued. "He lost his money during the depression and at one time he barely had enough money to meet his dentist's bill."

Josephine was born April 5, 1881, in Detroit to H. Kirke White and Amanda Cloistique Fortier. The family was wealthy, with interests in Acme Paint and Ferry Morse Seed companies, and they sent Josephine to a private school New York State. She married Lieutenant George L. Morrison of the 7th U.S. Cavalry, a graduate of West Point, in 1905. They had a son, George L. Morrison, the following year and in 1910, a daughter, Christine, who lived only a few months. They divorced and Josephine returned from Hawaii to Detroit, where she met Comstock.

Comstock, born July 2, 1877, in Alpena, graduated from the University of Michigan in 1899. By 1909 he'd become president of the State Savings Bank of Alpena, and from

Josephine was beautiful, with light brownish hair and brown eyes. She was only five feet tall and weighed 90 pounds. "Tiny, but couldn't be underestimated," Maryanne Comstock said. "William was a complete gentleman… a fascinating man… born in a suit with a white tie."

They married on April 22, 1919. She was 38 and he was a 41 year-old bachelor, so it was an adjustment when their son, William III, was born the year they were married. Comstock adopted her first son, changing his name to Kirke White Comstock.

"In private life he resides quietly in Ann Arbor with Mrs. Comstock and his two sons… " the *Michigan Manual* stated.[3] This didn't include the fact they had a chauffeur, upstairs maid, downstairs maid, and nursemaid to keep things running smoothly.

"They weren't very young to have a small child. She (Josephine) always said, 'Thank Goodness it was a male Comstock.' She could call him that and forget it," her daughter-in-law recalled.

"They sent young William to Culver Military Academy to get rid of him for the summer they were entertaining the National Governor's Conference on the (Mackinac) Island in 1934." Maryanne continued, "He got pneumonia and had to be brought back to the hospital in Ann Arbor, upsetting their plans.

"They had a very good life. They spent their summers apart." Maryanne mused. "And, they had a very good marriage, but they each went their own way." Josephine had summered at Nantucket Island, Massachusetts, from the time she was a child. She also spent many winters in Paris with her husband's sister, Marie Comstock.

Family members have told how Josephine was jolted when Comstock declared the 1933 banking holiday in Michigan and didn't tell her until he returned home that night. Josephine had a considerable amount of family money in banks and was upset to learn he'd closed them without a word to her. It was rumored that she never really forgave him for this.

Comstock moved to Detroit after his term as governor, where he and Josephine lived in the Tuller Hotel. He was elected as a nonpartisan candidate to the Detroit City Council in 1942 and served until his death.

Josephine and their son, William III, were reported to be with Comstock in an Alpena hospital when he died on June 16, 1949, and he was buried in Alpena. Kirke had died in 1947, but his son, Kirke White Comstock, Jr., of Albion, was at the funeral.

Josephine died in December 1955 and is buried in the White family plot, next to her daughter, Christine, in Elmwood Cemetery, Detroit.

William III and his wife, Maryanne, had three children: Christine Comstock, M.D., William Johnson Comstock, and Seth Comstock. ❖

William A. Comstock
State Archives

98

❖ Queena W. Fitzgerald ❖

Wife of

Governor Frank D. Fitzgerald

1935 and 1936, 1939 for two and one-half months

ueena Fitzgerald always did the things expected of her in the position of First Lady, but she never relished them. She was a homemaker and her family and her home were the major concerns of her life.

A very quiet, reserved and ladylike woman, her outside interests were the Garden Club, the ABC Club (a local woman's club), various women's groups of the Grand Ledge Congregational Church, and she was a life member of the Grand Ledge Order of the Eastern Star. During World War II she was very active in Red Cross work. She was also an avid gardener and a good bridge player.

Courtesy of Lorabeth Fitzgerald

She did not take part in her husband's political campaigns. During the time her husband was governor, however, he often counseled with her for her opinions on matters, according to their son, John Warner Fitzgerald.[1]

Queena Maud Warner, who disliked being called "Queenie," was born in Mulliken on October 14, 1889, to Mr. and Mrs. N. J. Warner. After graduating from Ferris Institute, she went to work as a secretary for the owner of the Grand Ledge Chair Company. In this small town, about 12 miles west of Lansing, she met Frank D. Fitzgerald. He was employed in the post office and had also attended Ferris Institute, although they had not known each other there. They were married in the home of her parents, June 28, 1909, and honeymooned in the new Ponchartrain Hotel in Detroit before settling in their Grand Ledge home.

Four years later, the couple moved to Lansing when Fitzgerald began working as a committee clerk for the Michigan Legislature there. They built a house there and in 1919, Fitzgerald was appointed deputy secretary of the state. But in 1920, he entered the business world as an officer in an Oldsmobile Distributing Corporation in Memphis, Tennessee. The dealership floundered, and in the spring of 1923 they returned to Grand Ledge and he became business manager of the State Highway Department in Lansing.[2]

Their only child, John Warner, was born in 1924. Queena was 35 and her husband was 39. She took motherhood very seriously. They tried to keep a normal, small-town upbringing for their son and did not entertain lavishly or travel extensively.

The family continued to reside in Grand Ledge when Fitzgerald was elected secretary of state and later governor. Young John went with his parents to special events, such as the Republican National Convention in Cleveland, Ohio, and the National Governor's Conference in 1936, in Biloxi, Mississipi. Otherwise their lives did not change much during this first term and returned to normal for two years after he was defeated in his bid for re-election in 1936.

Not about to give up, Fitzgerald made another bid for the governorship in 1938 and was victorious. Despite the urging of Queena to take better care of his health, the campaign was hard on him. Only 74 days after taking office, he died of a heart attack, on March 16, 1939. He was the only Michigan Governor to die while in office.[3]

Queena continued to live quietly in Grand Ledge until her death after a brief illness on May 15, 1970, at the age of 81. Both Queena and Fitzgerald were buried in the Oakwood Cemetery in Grand Ledge.

Their son, John W. Fitzgerald, became a state senator, a judge of the Court of Appeals, and served nine years on the Michigan Supreme Court before retiring as chief justice in 1983. He and his wife, Lorabeth, continue to live in the Fitzgerald home, where they raised their three sons: Frank M., Eric, and Adam. The house has been recognized as a Michigan historic site.[4]

Frank M. has followed in his grandfather's footsteps. He was elected to the MichiganHouse of Representatives in 1986 and represents the same district that his grandfather did. He has a daughter, Ellen, and a son named for his grandfather, John W. Fitzgerald.[5]

In the interest of clarity, the family line began in Grand Ledge with John Wesley Fitzgerald, who served one term in the Michigan Legislature (1895-96) and was the father of Governor Frank D. Fitzgerald. The Governor was the father of Justice John Warner Fitzgerald, who is father of Michigan Congressman Frank Moore Fitzgerald, who is father of John Wesley Fitzgerald. ❖

Frank D. Fitzgerald
State Archives

❖ Historical Note

From 1935 to 1941, Michigan's political parties played musical chairs. After serving one term, Republican Governor Fitzgerald was defeated by Democrat Frank Murphy. Two years later Fitzgerald was successful in his bid to defeat incumbent Murphy. Then, when Fitzgerald died after serving two and one-half months in office, Lieutenant Governor Luren D. Dickinson assumed the Office of Governor and served for a year and nine months. He failed in his bid for election, however, and Democrat Murray Van Wagoner was the victor.

This three-story, Fitzgerald house at 219 West Jefferson Avenue in Grand Ledge, is now a historical site and still the family residence.

❖ Marguerite Murphy Teahan ❖

Sister of

Governor Frank Murphy

1937 and 1938

Marguerite Murphy Teahan, sister of Governor Frank Murphy, served as hostess for him during the years he held positions in state and national government.

Marguerite was very pretty with dark hair and appeared slight or fragile. Although Murphy had two brothers, George and Harold, "Marguerite was a bit of a fanatic about Frank. She adored him," according to her niece, Denise Teahan Bancroft. "She loved serving as his hostess and was very good at it."

Marguerite was married to William Teahan of Windsor, Canada, and the couple accompanied Murphy as social aides in 1933 to the Philippine Islands. Murphy had been appointed governor-general and in 1935 was named United States High Commissioner to the Philippines.[1] As his official hostess, Marguerite became friends with President and Mrs. Manuel Luis Quezon. The Teahans adopted a daughter, Mary Aurora, and the Quezon's became her Godparents.[2]

When Murphy resigned to return to Michigan and become a candidate for governor of Michigan, the Teahans came too. They lived, as did Murphy, at the Whittier Hotel in Detroit. Following his election as governor, Marguerite was his hostess in Lansing.

Courtesy of Denise Bancroft

Frank Murphy
State Archives

Marguerite's niece recalls an instance when she was 5 years old: "I was out driving with Grandmother, my aunt, and a beautiful blonde actress was with us. She was wearing purple and had purple polish on her fingernails. I believe it was the motion picture star, Ann Harding, once linked romantically with Murphy.

"Women threw themselves at him (Murphy)," she continued. "He was charming… and a bachelor."[3] Having his married sister serve as his hostess must have provided a certain amount of protection for Murphy. Murphy's biographer, Sidney Fine, noted: "He (Murphy) was unusually attractive to women and craved their attention, but he loved his own career more."[4]

Murphy was defeated after one term as governor and President Franklin D. Roosevelt appointed him U.S. Attorney General. In 1940, he was appointed to the United States Supreme Court. The Teahans accompanied him to Washington, D.C. and Marguerite continued to serve as his hostess until he died. His death came unexpectedly on July 19, 1949, in Detroit.

Marguerite, George, Frank, and Harold J. Murphy were born in Harbor Beach, the children of John F. and Mary Murphy. John was a lawyer, a Democrat, and the family was Irish Catholic. Frank was born on April 13, 1890, and was buried in Rock Falls Cemetery, near Harbor Beach. His grave is in the corner of the cemetery with a cedar cross as a marker which reads, "Frank Murphy, Justice Supreme Court."[5] His father had wanted the simple marker and all members of the family have similar ones in the cemetery facing Lake Huron.

The Murphy home at Harbor Beach in Huron County, 1890. Frank and Marguerite lived here during their early childhood. It is now a public museum. State Archives

Marguerite was sick the last years of her life. She returned to Windsor and died there in 1962, in her seventies.[6] It is difficult to determine exact ages of the Murphys because Frank decided at some point in his career that he had been born in 1893, rather than 1890.[7] ❖

❖ **Historical Note**

During 1941 and 1942 a Frank Murphy served as lieutenant governor of Michigan and is sometimes confused with Governor Frank Murphy. The Governor was baptized as William Francis Murphy, but never used his first name; and therefore, had no middle initial to differentiate between the two men. The Lieutenant Governor had a wife, Constance Kirchner, and five children.

❖ Zora C. Dickinson ❖

Wife of

Governor Luren D. Dickinson

1939 and 1940

Zora Dickinson was ill most of the time Luren Dudley Dickinson was governor and was the only First Lady to die while her husband was in office. She died less than five months before he'd finished his term.

Dickinson had been elevated to the governorship because he was lieutenant governor when Governor Frank D. Fitzgerald died after serving only two and one-half months of his second term.

Zora, born in 1865 in Eaton Township, was a student of Dickinson's the first term he taught in a country school. When they met several years later, it was at a neighborhood church where she was a soloist, chorister, and organist. He was 24 and she was 18 years-old.

"At that time I had never heard anyone that could sing just like she did," he later wrote in his autobiography. "I think that I soon put in the background even the singing and it soon resulted in Zora Della Cooley, this young lady, becoming Mrs. Dickinson." On their 50th Wedding Anniversary, October 16, 1938, Dickinson said "...of all the high ideals that I anticipated in her 50 years before, there had been no disappointment, but as the years passed I saw new ones continually."[1]

Throughout the years Dickinson was very active politically. He served three terms in the Michigan House of Representatives, a term in the state senate, and seven times intermittently as lieutenant governor before moving into the governorship in 1939. He was also state vice president for the Woman's Suffrage Campaign and president of the Michigan Anti-Saloon League.

"In all these activities, the number one advisor was the lady at home, Mrs. Dickinson. I considered her advice far more valuable than that of the most eminent leaders in the state and never was disappointed."[2]

Zora preferred to remain quietly on their 250-acre farm three miles southeast of Charlotte, and didn't take part in any social affairs in Lansing. Every year while he was lieutenant governor, however, she invited the state senators to their farm for a fine dinner which she always cooked.

The Dickinson's were both very involved in church work all their lives. At one time, small but energetic Zora painted the outside of the local Methodist Church by herself. "She was afraid to get up on the steeple, so someone else painted it," a neighbor recalled. She taught Sunday School classes from early life until she had to give them up due to poor health in later years.

Although they had no children, the couple adopted a niece, Rilla Ethel, who died before Dickinson became governor. Ethel's brother, Verl Vinton, lived with them for several years.[3]

When Governor Dickinson was invited to attend former Governor Chase Osborn's Day in Sault Ste. Marie, he wrote on September 26, 1939: "It will be practically impossible for me to be present. I am making no dates or trips that will not permit me to be at home nights, because of Mrs. Dickinson's health. That must first be considered."

Another niece, Thelma Dickinson, took care of Zora in her last days of illness until her death on August 8, 1940. She was buried in Maple Hills Cemetery in Charlotte.[4]

Luren D. Dickinson
State Archives

That fall, Dickinson made a bid for re-election. "At 81, seeking a victory on his own, Dickinson hired a 61 year-old to run his campaign. Statehouse wags called it a youth movement. Dickinson was defeated by Murray D. Van Wagoner, a Democrat, in 1940."[5]

Dickinson died on April 22, 1943, and was buried beside Zora in the Charlotte Cemetery. ❖

❖ Historical Note

When Luren Dickinson was sworn into office as governor, it left the post of lieutenant governor vacant. Dickinson appointed Matilda Dodge Wilson to fill the position and she became the first woman to serve as lieutenant governor in the state of Michigan (See Michigan's Women Lieutenant Governors).

❖ Helen J. Van Wagoner ❖

Wife of

Governor Murray D. Van Wagoner

1941 and 1942

T he most difficult aspect of being a First Lady, Helen Van Wagoner recalled, was having her husband away from home so much.[1] Murray D. Van Wagoner had served as the state highway commissioner from 1933 until he took office as governor in 1941. During this time the Van Wagoners lived in several places in Lansing before buying a house on Everett Drive.

Van Wagoner was busy directing mobilization for World War II during his first year as governor. He immediately called the legislature into special session when Pearl Harbor was bombed.

"We didn't entertain much while he was in office," Helen said. "I was a Gray Lady. I did sewing and I liked to spend time at home."

Some friends described Helen as rather shy, but she considered herself an "even tempered" person. She also said she didn't think she had any special influence while her husband was in office.

"Influence," however, can be measured by various yardsticks in government circles. She was an excellent cook. She fed Murray's friends well and they all thought highly of her.[2]

An attractive brunette, Helen Josephine Jossman was born in Clarkston on April 19, 1898, and moved with her family to Pontiac while very young. She graduated from high school there and attended Pontiac Business College.

"Helen and Murray were high school sweethearts in Pontiac and the only dates they ever had were with each other. That was it!"[3]

Although Van Wagoner had been born in Kingston on March 18, 1898, he had moved to Oakland County when he was a small boy. His sister was Ether Van Wagoner Tufty, a nationally known newspaper correspondent in Washington, D.C.

Van Wagoner entered the University of Michigan and graduated in 1921 with an engineering degree. He was employed by the State Highway Department with headquarters in Alpena and he used Helen's Model A Ford for his surveying work.

Within a few years he started his own private engineering office in Pontiac and the couple made wedding plans.

Helen, who was a secretary/bookkeeper, and Van Wagoner were married on June 7, 1924, in a local funeral home. Helen's mother worked for the mortician and he allowed them to use the large room without cost.[4]

For seven years they lived a comparatively peaceful life in Pontiac, but always active "Pat" Van Wagoner was busy in politics. Although his family was Republican, in order to get a place on the ballot he had to run on the Democrat ticket. He made an unsuccessful bid for the Oakland County Surveyors Office in 1928.

Two years later, he was a successful candidate for county drain commissioner and served two terms. During this time their two daughters were born; Ellen Louise and Jo Ann. By 1933 he was a candidate on the state Democrat ticket, and was elected to the office of state highway commissioner. The family moved to Lansing while he served two, four-year terms as highway commissioner and continued to live there after he was elected governor in November of 1940.

Van Wagoner served one term. He lost his bid for re-election and the family moved to Birmingham. He made another unsuccessful bid for the governorship in 1946, and in 1947 was appointed by President Harry S. Truman as director of U.S. Military Government of Bavaria. In 1949 he was named land commissioner of Bavaria for the U.S. State Department.

Helen and Jo Ann accompanied him to Bavaria during these two years, but Ellen stayed here as she was a student at the University of Michigan. Helen liked Bavaria. "I liked the people – they were so wonderful; and the country was beautiful," she said later.

During this time they all went boar hunting and brought the mounted trophies back with them. "Murray's boar tusks are still hanging in the Detroit Club," his son-in-law, Walter Wikol said.

"She was a very gentle lady, but she did surprise you," Wikol said when asked if hunting wasn't a bit out of character for Helen. "When we played lawn croquet with her, she beat the socks off everyone." The family loved to play dominoes and were very good at it, too.

When they returned to Birmingham, Van Wagoner was a consulting engineer and vice president of a Ferndale door manufacturing company. He also filled out a term on the University of Michigan Board of Regents in 1951, by appointment, but failed to win a seat in the next election.

Murray D. Van Wagoner
State Archives

Although she was asked for a photograph, Helen did not supply one for use in the 1977 edition of *First Ladies of Michigan* and none could be found. Van Wagoner, however, called the author about 6:00 a.m. one November morning in 1984, to say he would send a photo of his wife. Along with it, he wrote: "If you revise or bring your book up-to-date, I would like you to run a picture of Mrs. Van Wagoner. I am enclosing one that might do."

They were both 86 at this time and they had always been very close. He was still looking out for her. Helen died of cancer on April 22, 1986, in Botsford General Hospital of Farmington Hills, two days after her 88th birthday. If she had lived until June 7, the couple would have marked their 62nd Wedding Anniversary. Van Wagoner died seven weeks later, at the age of 88. Both were buried in White Chapel Memorial Cemetery of Troy.[5]

They were survived by their daughters. Ellen (who died in 1988) was married to Walter Wikol of Birmingham, and they had four children: Murray D. Van Wagoner Wikol, Michael, Amy Christine, and Thomas. Murray lives today in the Van Wagoner family home in Birmingham. Jo Ann, who lives in Reno, Nevada, with her husband, U.S. Army General (Retired) Frederick Karhohs, has two children: Major Jeffrey Karhohs and James Karhohs, DDS. ❖

Helen with Governor "Pat" Van Wagoner and their two daughters, Jo Ann and Ellen. Bentley

❖ Anne O. Kelly ❖

Wife of

Governor Harry F. Kelly

1943 through 1946

 permanent summer home was purchased by the state for Michigan's Governors on Mackinac Island in 1945, during Anne Kelly's years as First Lady. The National Governor's Conference was scheduled to take place there that summer and in order to get the house ready, it was staffed with inmates from state penitentiaries.

Although furnishings were quite complete, new organdy curtains were purchased for the many windows. Anne and two other women sewed steadily for three days to assure their fit and finished in time to open the house to visiting governors and their wives.[1]

Handling a crisis was nothing new for Anne. She was the mother of six children, ranging from 2 to 13 years of age when her husband, Harry F. Kelly, took the Office of Governor in January of 1943. Their immediate problem was moving from Detroit into a house in Lansing large enough to accommodate the entire family. This was solved by buying a large, older house near the Capitol and converting the third floor ballroom into rooms for the three oldest boys.

Because of the war, full time domestic help was almost impossible to find to help manage a very busy household and help entertain. So Anne had to make do with a mother's helper during the days and a cook who came in from 5:00 p.m. to 7:00 p.m. daily. [2]

Anne Veronica O'Brien was born on December 3, 1905, in Laurium, located in the Upper Peninsula. Her parents were Michael E. and Nell Harrington O'Brien and her uncle was Judge Patrick H. O'Brien. They were all Democrats. Her father had established a bank in Laurium, but the family moved to Detroit when she was about 5 years old where he established an insurance company.

Anne attended Detroit Parochial High School and graduated from Sargent School for Physical Education in Cambridge, Massachusetts. Returning to Detroit, she taught physical education at Girl's Catholic Central High School. She met Kelly when she went to a bridge party at the home of her sister and they were married a year later.

Kelly, born in Ottowa, Illinois, on April 19, 1895, had attended Notre Dame Law School until he enlisted in 1917 in World War I. He went to France as a second lieutenant and suffered wounds that cost him a leg. He was awarded the croix de guerre.[3] After the war, he took up the practice of law in Illinois where he was elected state's attorney in LaSalle County and served a four-year term. In 1924, he moved to Michigan to join his father and brother in their law firm in Detroit.

Anne had naturally curly auburn hair, was five feet and seven inches tall, very athletic and a marvelous dancer. She and Kelly were married on May 4, 1929, and her family was upset when she married a Republican, but they were both Catholic and that eased the pain.

During the next 12 years the couple had six children: Joanne (Mrs. Louis T. Hagopian), Harry F. Jr., Brian J., Lawrence M., Roger J., and Mary (Mrs. Thomas F. James).

Meanwhile, Kelly became involved in Michigan politics and spent most of the rest of his life in public service. He was appointed assistant prosecuting attorney in Wayne County in 1930, named manager of the Detroit Office of the Michigan Liquor Control Commission in 1935, elected secretary of state in 1938 and re-elected in 1940. In 1942, Kelly was elected governor and re-elected in 1944.[4]

Anne didn't take part in many social events during her husband's four years as World War II Governor and was rarely seen in his office. "I took part in many club activities before I was married," she was quoted as saying. "Now I feel it is up to me to keep the household running smoothly. It isn't fair for a husband to be met at the door with a recital of problems every night."

Keeping things running smoothly wasn't any easy job. Visitors to the Kelly home described it as resembling a railroad station or the starting gate at a race track. The children naturally got a lot of attention, but she concentrated on seeing they did all the things that other children were doing, adding firmly, "and we are going to keep it that way."

In addition to efficiently running the family and the household, Anne was the Governor's social manager. She gained a reputation for her warm, friendly manner and her ability to immediately put people at ease. "She had a talent for making everything look so easy, whether entertaining five or 50 visitors," according to her daughter, Mary. "Visitors have always been assured of warm hospitality and excellent food at her table."

Anne recalled the time Kelly invited ten legislators to come for dinner and they had mentioned they'd like to have Italian spaghetti, which they'd enjoyed previously. Everything went along well, dinner was served and then

Harry Kelly
State Archives

they waited and waited. Finally, Anne went out to see why no one had come in to clear the table and discovered the cook had gone home when she'd finished her 5:00 to 7:00 p.m. shift. The embarrassed hostess returned to tell the legislators what had happened. They trooped into the kitchen, helped cut pies and served themselves. "They all had a good time," she laughed. "But they kidded me about it a lot, later."

Although the wife of the Governor was not expected to take an active role in governmental decisions, Anne participated fully in all aspects of Kelly's life. "Her opinions were sought and her quiet guidance and advice were influential," her daughter pointed out.

For a few fairly quiet years after Kelly decided not to run for a third term, he returned to his law practice. But he made another try for governor in 1950 and lost by only 1,154 votes. In 1953 he was elected a justice of the Michigan Supreme Court. Kelly continued in public life and the couple lived in Birmingham until he retired in January of 1971. Just six weeks later on February 8, 1971, he died from a massive stroke while they were in Florida, and was buried in Southfield.

Since then Anne has spent her time working for the Catholic Church, reading, knitting, and being creative in her kitchen. "She has a sense of humor which never seems to fail her. She has unending patience with her children and grandchildren. And she has a curiosity about life and living which has kept her young," her daughter said. "Although she has a quiet and unassuming manner, she is the true hub of the family."

Technically, she makes her home with her daughter, Mary, in Saginaw, but is seldom there. She spends her winters in Florida and her summers at the isolated cabin on a lake near Gaylord, which has always been a favorite family place. She also has 17 grandchildren and six great-grandchildren to enjoy and keep her occupied. ❖

The Kelly clan (left to right): Roger, Mary, Anne, Joanne, Governor Harry Kelly, Larry, and twins: Harry Jr. and Brian.

❖ Mae P. Sigler ❖

Wife of

Governor Kim Sigler

1947 and 1948

Their lives together started romantically, but ended separately and tragically. Mae Pierson was a nursing student and Kim Sigler was in pre-law at the University of Michigan in Ann Arbor when they met. Mae and another co-ed were paddling on the Huron River when their canoe capsized. Sigler was drifting along in his canoe and reading a text book when he heard their screams. The girls were in the water and Mae couldn't swim. Sigler came to their rescue.[1]

An active and attractive girl, Mae Louise Pierson was born on December 11, 1893, and raised on her parents large farm near Goodrich, a small town southeast of Flint. She had a brother, E. J. and a sister, Bess. After graduating from high school, Mae entered the University of Michigan to study nursing.[2]

Sigler, born in Schuyler, Nebraska, on May 2, 1894, was the son of cattle ranchers Daniel and Bertha Zeigler. He had a younger sister, Goldie. During the first World War, persons with German last names anglicized them, so Kimber Cornellus Zeigler became Kim Sigler. He'd decided to be a lawyer and after graduating from high school he went to the University of Michigan in 1913. It was during his two years here that he met Mae.[3]

In 1915 Sigler transferred to the University of Detroit Law School so he could better finance his education by working nights in the Highland Park plant of the Ford Motor Company. Mae completed work on her Registered Nurse degree and they were married on November 11, 1917. They set up housekeeping at 155 Grand Avenue in Highland Park, and she worked in the office of Dr. Rolland Parmieter.[4]

After Sigler graduated from law school in 1918, he worked for several law firms in Detroit. Their first daughter, Betty, was born here on August 3, 1919. The couple dreamed of living in a small city and they spent their weekends visiting possible places in Michigan for Sigler to practice. When they discovered Hastings, they immediately liked the town. They moved there in 1922, and stayed for nearly a quarter of a century.

112

Although it was the Siglers who had adopted Hastings, the townspeople returned their feeling and quickly accepted the handsome young couple. Women found young Sigler good-looking, with a colorful personality; and men considered Mae as someone special.[5]

Soon after the couple arrived in Hastings, the Democrats offered Sigler the chance to run on their ticket for Barry County Prosecuting Attorney. Sigler ran, won and was re-elected two times. He needed the money as he was starting his practice and soon built a reputation as an effective prosecutor. His interest in politics continued but philosophically he was closer to the Republican party and he eventually joined their ranks.

Sigler always had a reputation for being a snappy dresser. Mae told of ironing a crease in a different place on his pants when they looked a little worn, during the first lean years of his law practice. When he was governor, he showed a reporter his suits at the Hotel Olds in Lansing. Estimates have ranged from 45 to 73 hanging in a closet.

Two more daughters were born to the Siglers in Hastings; Beverly in 1923 and Goldie Madalon, four years later. The first tragedy struck when 11 year-old Beverly developed infantile paralysis at their summer home on Gun Lake and died within a few days.

As the years passed, they joined the country club and had a beautiful home on Green Street. Sigler's law office was so elegantly furnished that people came just to look at the place.

Virginia Baird, East Lansing, who lived across the street from the Siglers and baby-sat for them, recalls that Mae was a generous, kind person. "My father had died when I was young and Mrs. Sigler made dresses for me."

Sigler was elected district governor of the 151st Rotary International and Mae accompanied him to a 1937 convention in Europe. They toured 11 countries. In 1943 he joined a law firm in Battle Creek, but later that year he was appointed special prosecutor of the Ingham County Grand Jury to clean up graft and corruption in state government. His success lead to his being elected governor less than four years later.[6]

Mae was ahead of her time with her opinions on women's liberation. She was quoted as saying she wouldn't die happy until a man had to go through a pregnancy and childbirth. With the onset of multiple sclerosis, Mae developed an ataxia and there were some unfounded rumors that she had a drinking problem.[7]

Sigler told a reporter-friend that not long after Beverly's death, he noticed his wife was not speaking clearly and he was impatient with her. Then it developed that she

Kim Sigler
State Archives

113

was suffering from multiple sclerosis and he spent thousands of dollars trying to find a cure for her.

By the time Sigler was elected governor, Mae was confined to a wheelchair by the disease and rarely attended public affairs. Despite her illness, Mae's sense of humor did not fail her. They lived in a suite at the Hotel Olds, across from the Capitol, so "she'd never be without any service she needed," Sigler said. But she loved Mackinac Island and they stayed there during the summers.

The Howard Sobers were good friends of the couple and this may have influenced them to donate their home for use as the Governor's Residence more than two decades later.

Sigler's daughter, Madalon, was a student at Michigan State University and lived with her parents in the hotel during her senior year.

"I went with Father to more functions than Mother did. She was sick and didn't participate much, except for a few reception lines," she recalled, adding, "Mother had 'lots of spizerinktum' as my Dad would say." Madalon later married a Lansing attorney, Richard Gossett, and they moved to McAlester, Oklahoma.

When Sigler failed to win re-election in 1948, he formed a law firm with a Lansing attorney. On November 30, 1953, the plane he was piloting crashed near Battle Creek, killing him and three passengers. Killed with Sigler were Ruth Prentice, a divorcee, who had been his secretary for some 20 years, her sister, and her sister's husband.

Mae was spending time with her daughter, Betty (Mrs. Byron Slattery), in California when the accident occurred. Her granddaughter, Beverly, was 6 years old and recalls that Mae was very upbeat and had lots of zest. "She smoked with a long, sterling engraved cigarette holder," she said. "I liked her."

After Sigler's death, Mae and Betty, also a victim of multiple sclerosis, lived in the Hotel Olds in Lansing until 1959. Ken McCormick, *Detroit Free Press* staff writer described her as "one of those rare individuals who can smile from a wheelchair and say pleasant things, though it often was difficult to understand her (due to the disease). Her greatest disappointment was not being able to help Kim in the campaign that made him Governor.

"It was heartbreaking to see Mae guiding her way in and out of the hotel drugstore in a wheelchair. She had lost considerable weight, But she hung on. She and Betty helped each other as best they could, each becoming more helpless as the years went by," McCormick wrote.

Finally, Mae accepted Madalon's invitation to live with her in Oklahoma and she spent the last five years of her life there. She died on October 22, 1963, at the age of 69, and was buried in the family plot beside Sigler and their second daughter in

Hastings' Riverside Cemetery, overlooking the Thornapple River. She was survived by their two daughters and five grandchildren.[9] Betty died in 1977 and was buried in California.

On May 1, 1987, a Michigan Memorial marker was dedicated to Governor Sigler, the only governor to call Barry County his home. The ceremonies were attended by granddaughter, Beverly Slattery Ciciliano, and great-grandson, Luke Ciciliano, from Las Vegas, Nevada. Daniel Brooke Gossett, a grandson of Sigler's from Tulsa, Oklahoma, was a speaker during the ceremonies. ❖

Virginia Baird (left) and Maureen Ketchum beside Sigler's Historical Marker placed in Hastings in 1987.

❖ Nancy Q. Williams ❖

Wife of

Governor G. Mennen Williams

1949 to 1960

ancy Williams was a popular governor's wife during the 12 years she was First Lady. People in all walks of life identified with her outgoing, friendly nature and the couple became familiar figures, "Nancy and Soapy." Somewhat ironically, she was the governor's wife most comfortable in high society circles since Josephine White Comstock in 1933 to 1934.

Daniel Lace Quirk, Jr., and Julia Trowbridge Quirk were her parents. Her father was president of the Peninsular Paper Company and president of a bank in Ypsilanti. Nancy Lace Quirk, born on June 12, 1915, had two brothers and a sister, all several years older.

When her brother, Daniel T., was elected mayor of Ypsilanti, Nancy had her first taste of the political process. Because there was a 12 year age difference between the two, people often assumed she was the Mayor's daughter.

Following her high school years in Ypsilanti, Nancy graduated from the Masters School at Dobbs Ferry in New York, and then entered the University of Michigan's School of Social Work.

Gerhard Mennen Williams was born in Detroit to a wealthy family on February 23, 1911. His mother was Elma Mennen of a toiletries fortune which provided his nickname, "Soapy." He earned his A.B. degree at Princeton University and graduated from the University of Michigan Law School in 1936. He, too, had been raised in a family with a history of Republicanism, but decided to be a Democrat while in law school.

The couple met in 1935, Williams graduated in 1936, and they were married the next year, June 26, 1937, a few weeks after Nancy received her degree. They lived in Washington, D.C., where he held several federal government positions. Governor

Frank Murphy, a friend who had been an attorney for Williams' parents, was influential in steering him and advising him toward jobs advancing his political career.[1]

Williams was in the General Counsel's Unit of the Office of Price Administration (OPA) when their son, Gerhard Mennen Jr., "Gery," was born in 1941. In 1942, Williams began a four year stint with the United States Navy. He earned ten battle stars in the Pacific theater and emerged as lieutenant commander in 1946.

During the war years, Nancy served as a member of the Red Cross Canteen Corps in Washington, D.C., and then transferred to the Motor Corps to drive for the Canteen. She returned to Ypsilanti in 1943 when their second child, Nancy Quirk, was born and continued her volunteer work. She drove army trucks to the Fairgrounds in Detroit with the Motor Corps and spent two years as a Red Cross Nurses' Aide.

When Williams returned from the war, he became Deputy OPA Director in Michigan. The couple's third child, Wendy Stock, was born in 1946. The next year Governor Kim Sigler appointed him to the Liquor Control Commission, and in 1948 Williams decided the time was ripe to make a bid for the governorship on the Democrat's ticket.

Nancy and "Soapy" began a political partnership that continued for the rest of their lives. Beginning their campaign from Ypsilanti, they rallied support from thousands of voting veterans. Many were going to universities on the G.I. Bill and living in nearby Willow Run Village.

Williams had not yet inherited his fortune, so they mortgaged their house and set out to win the election. They toured the state in a dilapidated DeSoto with Nancy usually at the wheel. "Soapy" wore a green and white polka-dot bow tie that became his trademark and frequently called square dances while on the victorious campaign trail.

"Martha Griffiths and I started the tea programs, from home to home, so we began to get women involved in politics and as candidates," Nancy recalls.[2]

One of the trials Nancy discovered after Williams won the election "was finding a large home, comfortable enough for a family of five and not too big to run with little domestic help and no secretarial help." She would have liked to have moved into a Governor's Mansion, she said at the time. "On the other hand, I'm happy we can bring up our children in our own home… on our property. It's probably a more normal life for youngsters than that if they were living in an official mansion."[3]

G. Mennen Williams
State Archives

Their solution was to rent a big, white house on Main Street in Lansing, "where they lived with their three children, several Cocker Spaniels, Wendy's guppies, and a devoted housekeeper."[4] Two years later they purchased a larger house, the same one that former Governor Chase S. Osborn had rented years previously.

"We had some wonderful years and some wonderful experiences... and we enjoyed it all," she said later. "We used the Governor's Summer Residence on Mackinac Island hard for 12 years." They liked it so much, in fact, that they bought a large house of their own, overlooking the Straits of Mackinac, in 1959.

Between attending meetings and doing family chores, such as marketing and carting children around to their activities, she managed to wear out three cars during Williams' terms in office. "It was difficult, because I had no secretary... the Governor's salary was very low," she said. Nancy also had a personal battle in 1958 when she put up a valiant struggle and overcame a bout with Guillain-Barre syndrome.

"Soapy and I talked all the government issues over, all the time," she recalls. "The problems then were mental health, schools, and social problems."

Nancy's deep interest in the health field and nursing has continued through the years. She was a member of Junior Auxiliary of Sparrow Hospital, 1949 to 1960; served on the board of Michigan League for Nursing; on the board of the National Association for Practical Nurse Education; on the National Advisory Council for Nursing for the U.S. Department of Health, Education, and Welfare; and served in many other capacities dealing with nurses and practical nurses.

The former First Lady's list of volunteer works range from being a Cub Scout and Brownie leader to that of being Michigan State Chairman for Muscular Dystrophy from 1954 to 1960. She has been active in numerous organizations, including the Woman's National Farm and Garden Club, American Association of University Women, National Association of Social Workers, Daughters of the American Revolution, YWCA, VFW Auxiliary – Post 995, and a member of the Board of Trustees, Founders Society of the Detroit Institute of Arts.

Honorary degrees of Doctor of Laws have been awarded to her by Eastern Michigan University and Wayne State University. During the years Williams was assistant secretary of state for African Affairs, 1961 to 1966, the couple lived in Washington and made about four trips annually to Africa. They spent their free time looking for and amassing a large collection of African art. While Williams was the United States Ambassador to the Philippines, 1968 to 1969, they searched for Chinese porcelain. They donated these to various colleges and universities in the state and gave a major collection to the Detroit Institute of Arts.

The couple returned from Washington to their Grosse Pointe Farms home in 1970 and Williams was elected to the Michigan Supreme Court that fall. Nancy accompanied him to Lansing when court was in session and spent her time enjoying reunions with friends in the area and playing bridge or golf. He was re-elected eight years later and was chief justice before retiring in 1986.

To celebrate their 50th Wedding Anniversary on June 26, 1987, the couple took all their children to Bermuda: Gery, with his wife, Lannie, and their children Lee Ann and G. Mennen III; Nancy, with husband Theodore Ketterer III and their children – Julie, Jenny and Lucy; Wendy, with husband Michael Burns, and their children – Rebecca, Bradley, and Nancy.

Although still active in Episcopalian Church work, life for the Williams' was comparatively quiet after leading such busy lives f or so many years. Then, on February 2, 1988, the former Governor suffered a massive cerebral hemorrhage and died several hours later. He was buried in the cemetery on Mackinac Island.

Nancy has continued living in their beautiful home with a view overlooking Lake St. Clair. She sorted the Governor's mementoes and gave all his papers to the Michigan Historical Collections, Bentley Historical Library, University of Michigan. In June of 1989, Nancy married James Gram, a lawyer and a longtime family friend. Although she doesn't travel as much as previously, she enjoys working in her garden and is still serving on various boards, including the Detroit Institute of Arts in Detroit.[5] ❖

The Williams family, 1981.
Center: Nancy and Justice G. Mennen Williams. Left front: Theodore Ketterer III and NancyJulie, Jenny, and Lucy. Right standing: Gery, Lee Ann, Lannie, Gery III. Far left front: Wendy and Michael Burns, Rebecca, Bradley, and Nancy.

Alice N. Swainson

Wife of

Governor John B. Swainson

1961 and 1962

Although Alice Swainson was First Lady for only two years, she had been through more political campaigns than most of her predecessors by the time her husband was sworn into the Governor's Office.

John Swainson had served as state senator for four years and as lieutenant governor two years, prior to his election as governor. Alice was therefore familiar with the political jungle, but always kept a low profile. A genuine and very likeable person, she gives the impression to friends that she is just as happy being a homemaker as she was to be a First Lady.

The daughter of Martin and Vera Nielsen, Alice was born in Detroit on March 31, 1927. Her father owned the Raymond Tool and Dye Corporation in Detroit. She was the third of their four children, having an older brother, older sister, and a younger sister. After graduating from Mackenzie High School, she entered Olivet College to major in music and study voice.

Alice's life changed direction when she was a sophomore. She met John Burley Swainson. He immediately appreciated the slender girl with blue eyes, blonde hair, and a beautiful voice. Despite the fact that there were 76 women and only four men enrolled in the war-time college, it was Alice that John began to date.[1]

The son of John A. C. and Edna May Burley Swainson, John B. was born on July 31, 1925, in Windsor, Ontario. When he was 9 months old his parents moved with him to Port Huron where he was raised. He graduated from Port Huron High School, became a U.S. citizen, and enlisted in the army at age 18, as soon as he was eligible.

While overseas with the 95th Infantry Division under General George S. Patton, in November 1944, a mine blast left him with only one leg and that had to be amputated at a field hospital. He spent the next 14 months in hospitals and his final convalescence was at Percy Jones Hospital, near Battle Creek. It was also near Olivet College and he enrolled there in 1946.

After dating during the school year, Alice and John were married in Lansing on July 21, 1946, and in the fall they both returned to campus life.

In a toboggan accident that winter, Swainson was injured and had to have a leg re-amputated. He was advised to live in a location where there was no snow, so the young couple moved to Chapel Hill, North Carolina. Here he continued his undergraduate work and entered law school at the University of North Carolina.

Their first two children were born during this time: John Stephen, on August 16, 1947, and Hans Peter, on

John B. Swainson
State Archives

121

December 13, 1949. Like other veterans and their wives throughout the nation, the Swainsons survived on the G.I. Bill and Alice was too busy at home to complete work on her degree.

About six months after his graduation in 1951, Alice had to have a lung operation, so they returned to Michigan and Swainson practiced law in Detroit. They first lived in Redford Township and then moved to Plymouth.

Interested in politics from his college days, Swainson was elected to the state senate from his district in 1954 and re-elected in 1956. They built a home in Plymouth that year and he commuted by train to Lansing. Their daughter, Kristina Ann, was born on October 15, 1958. A month later, Swainson was elected lieutenant governor to Governor G. Mennen Williams, and in 1960 was elected governor. They then moved to Lansing.

"I had to find a place to live there and I was busy. Stephen was 13, Peter was 11, and Kristine was a 2 year-old," Alice recalled. "It was a good experience for them."[2]

"When we had visiting dignitaries we put them up in our home," she continued. "I did all the grocery shopping and cooking, but we were fortunate to have a housekeeper."

"There were no appropriations for entertainment at that time either," she said. For the Swainsons, this was a serious drawback. They always lived on his salaries and his disability pension from the army. They had no independent wealth to fall back on, as many governors had.

Did Alice have much influence on the Governor? "Husbands and wives do talk about things," Swainson answered. "We had young children and her interests were primarily in the family and the household. But she certainly filled social obligations."[3]

Actually, any spare time Alice could manage was spent campaigning every two years for her husband. The gubernatorial term did not extend to four years until after the 1963 Michigan Constitution was adopted.

When Swainson lost his bid for re-election in 1962, he practiced law in Detroit and they bought a 163-acre farm near Manchester two years later. "We decided to settle someplace within an hours drive from both Detroit and Lansing," Alice explained. "We'd always liked the Manchester area, especially the rolling hills we'd seen during campaigns in the fall."

Swainson was elected as Wayne County Circuit Court Judge in 1965, and in 1969 the family sold their house in Plymouth and moved to their farm with its rambling, renovated homestead, "The Hustings."

In 1970, Swainson was elected to the Michigan Supreme Court and served for five years until he resigned under a cloud. He had been accused of accepting a bribe to arrange a new trial for a convicted burglar who had turned informant for the F.B.I. He was acquitted of the bribery charge but sentenced for perjury by a petit jury because he said he did not remember two telephone calls he'd made 33 months prior to his appearance before the grand jury.[4] His license to practice law was suspended for three years and these were very difficult times for the Swainsons.

At age 50, Swainson had served in the all three branches of state government but now found himself stripped of his career. "I became an antique dealer and enjoyed the challenge of following history through the discovery of the furnishings and artifacts of earlier times," he recalled.[5] This experience helped prepare him for an appointment in 1985 to the Michigan Historical Commission and in later years he became president of the commission.

"Without Alice, everything that I have accomplished would have been without meaning," he said in a 1988 Founder's Day Address at Olivet College.[6] And he still insists she is the prettiest First Lady of them all.

With their children grown, Alice enjoys painting and is active in the Chelsea Painters group, the Ann Arbor Women's Painters, and is a member of the Michigan Watercolor Society. In community affairs she serves as a juror in local art shows and has been on the United Way Board. She takes voice lessons, sings in the choir and, participates in work for the local Emanuel Church of Christ with her husband.

Their daughter, Kristina Ann, lives in Manchester with her husband, Louis Way, and their two children: Andrew Louis, who was born on September 30, 1986; and Allyson Kristina, who was born May 6, 1990. Their son, John Stephen, lives in Santa Fe, New Mexico, and their youngest son, Hans, lives in Connecticut.

"I'm busy being a grandmother," Alice said in November 1992, commenting on how nice it was to have her daughter living nearby. She was planning to leave shortly to drive her 95 year-old mother to Florida.

Friends of the Swainsons say they lead a contented, purposeful life today, and add "They deserve it." ❖

The Swainson home, "The Hustings," near Manchester.

❖ Lenore L. Romney ❖

Wife of

Governor George W. Romney

1963 - 1969

ather frail in appearance, but strong in spirit, Lenore Romney has always done her best to make this a better world. After raising the four Romney children to be good citizens, she traveled around the state exhorting college students to have high morals, and then set out to solve the nation's problems by promoting volunteerism.

That sounds like a big order, but Lenore is not one to shrink from a mission. When she rises to speak to an audience her cheeks flush slightly and she starts talking intently. She delivers a message with such inspiration that her listeners virtually march out of the room ready to fight for righteouness and defeat all evil.

Some of this spirit is undoubtedly inherited from a maternal grandmother, Rosetta Berry Robison, who walked with a handcart company from Reading, Michigan, to Salt Lake Valley when she was only 14 years old. Rosetta was left a widow with three children and the youngest, Alma, was Lenore's mother. Alma graduated from Utah State Agricultural College in Logan, Utah, where she met Harold LaFount. They married and had four daughters: Elsie, Lenore, Constance, and Ruth, in that order.

Lenore was born in Logan on November 9, 1909, and was a 4 year-old when the family moved to Salt Lake City. She had a happy childhood in a home with strong guidelines.

"Mother was brought up to believe the man was the head of the house. I never heard her speak crossly or contradict my father in my life," Lenore recalled. She added with a laugh, "That is not the way I am at all."[1]

George Wilcken Romney was born on July 8, 1907, one of six boys and a girl in the family of Gaskell and Anna Amelia Pratt Romney. When he was a 5 year-old they moved from Colonia Dublan, Mexico, to Texas, then to California, on to Idaho, and later to Utah. He met Lenore in Salt Lake City's Latter-Day Saints University High School.

By the time they graduated, George had begun a courtship that eventually took him across the continent seven times. Lenore left with her parents for Washington, D.C. when her father was appointed to the Federal Radio Commission by President Calvin Coolidge. She recalls how her father bought a new pin-striped morning suit especially to wear when he met the President and then all Silent Cal said to him was, "When in doubt, read the law. Good morning."

George W. Romney
State Archives

While in Washington, Lenore graduated from George Washington University in three years because her parents had promised she could attend the American

125

Laboratory School of the Theatre in New York when she'd completed her degree. Meanwhile, Romney found a job in Washington working for Senator David I. Walsh of Massachusetts as his tariff specialist, so he could be near Lenore.

By the time Lenore left to study in New York, Romney had begun training as an apprentice for Alcoa Aluminum Company in Pittsburgh. He made weekend trips to see her. She was offered a contract with MGM and went to Hollywood in 1930. After a few months, she was offered a three year contract with the studio, but by then Romney had managed to get a company transfer to California. He convinced her to marry him and she turned down the film offer.

On July 2, 1931, the Romney's were married in the Salt Lake City Temple of Latter-Day Saints. They returned to his $125 a month job in California for a few months and then he transferred back to Washington with the aluminum company. Their two daughters were born there: Lynn, on June 6, 1935, and Jane, on March 18, 1938.

The family moved to Detroit in 1939, when Romney became manager for the Automobile Manufacturers Association. Here their first son, George Scott, was born on June 7, 1941, and Willard Mitt, on March 12, 1947. Lenore devoted her time to raising their four children.

In 1948, Romney started working for the Nash-Kelvinator Corporation and helped arrange a merger with the Hudson Motor Car Company to form the American Motors Corporataion (AMC). He became president and chairman of AMC in 1954 and turned the money-losing companies around financially.

Romney created Citizens for Michigan in 1959, a bipartisan group that later spearheaded the drive for a Constitutional Convention. The Romney children were now old enough, so Lenore could spend more time working at his side. When the convention was called in 1960, Romney held his first elective office as a delegate and was elected one of the three vice presidents.

Lenore was a frequent visitor to the convention in Lansing. She became so familiar with the proposed revised constitution that she could confidently work for its adoption. It was approved by voters and in 1962 Romney resigned from American Motors to run for governor. Lenore hit the campaign trail simultaneously with his travels and her talks throughout the state played a significant role in his successful election that fall.

Concerned about the problems mounting on college campuses, Lenore continued to travel and talk to young people while Romney was governor. She made more than 1,000 speeches, as many as eight a day, primarily to students. Always she stressed the importance of a strong family life. "No success, no matter what, can compensate for failure in the home," she'd point out. "We (women) can't be happy in our achievements if we have failed personally in our homes with our husbands and our children. This, I think, is being lost sight of."

"I've always had a lot to say," she explained. "But no one paid any attention until George was governor." Hectic as her schedule was, she confided that she'd rather be giving speeches than mopping floors at home.

Romney was re-elected to another two-year term and in 1966 to a four-year term as specified in the new constitution. Meanwhile, the Romneys rented a house in East Lansing and Lenore had a volunteer secretary, Mary Browder, to help with her correspondence and scheduling.

Only a week after his third inauguration, Lenore was flying in a small plane enroute to give a talk when one engine sputtered and died out. The pilot managed to make a bumpy landing in an open field. He arranged for a car to come and pick her up so she arrived on time for her speaking engagement. Only a handful of people ever knew about the incident. "It would have embarrassed the pilot," she explained.

In 1966, Romney made a bid for the U.S. Presidency. Lenore again followed a strenuous schedule campaigning for him, this time on a nation-wide tour. While she was tramping through snow in Wisconsin, word came that he had withdrawn from the race. Typically, she let it be known that she should have been consulted first.

Although Romney was notorious for his strong will and finger-pointing directness, Lenore referred to him as "intense" and he listened to her when she had a strong opinion of her own. Elly Peterson, the first woman to become state chairman of either political party in Michigan, worked with both of them. "They had something very special," she observed.

When Richard Nixon took office as President in 1969, he appointed Romney as Secretary of Housing and Urban Development (HUD). Romney resigned as governor and headed for Washington. Lenore moved their furnishings from Lansing to their condominium in Washington's Shoreham West.

Before she'd left Michigan, Lenore had been named to the board of the National Center for Voluntary Action, a committee to mobilize volunteers for problem solving in communities. She spent much of the next year back in the state, however, campaigning for a seat in the U.S. Senate. She had been drafted by Republican party leaders as a "consensus" candidate, but it was an unsuccessful attempt. She'd long promoted the election of women to high political offices, but the state voters weren't ready yet for that giant step.

In Washington, Lenore occasionally attended cabinet meetings as an onlooker. "We couldn't speak during the sessions, but afterwards the cabinet members would answer our questions," she said. She also traveled tirelessly around the nation helping establish volunteer action centers, often with other cabinet wives.

A highlight during Romney's years with HUD was a month long trip they took to study Housing and Urban Development in Spain, Portugal, France, Germany, and England. In England they were invited at attend Queen Elizabeth's annual Garden

Party and were among 50 of the 6,000 guests invited to hold private conversations in her royal tent. "It was just fantastic," Lenore reported. "She (the Queen) is beautiful, alert, and very aware of England's problems."

Romney resigned from his cabinet post in February of 1973, prior to the Watergate incident, and the couple returned to their home in Bloomfield Hills. Although demands on their time were less stringent, they continued at a fast pace. Lenore served on the National Council for the Prevention of Child Abuse, on the National Board for Volunteers in Justice and Criminal Justice, and lectured nation-wide as a Woodrow Wilson Fellow.

In July of 1978, Lenore was hospitalized twice with an irregular heartbeat, but it slowed her down only temporarily. Four years later, she was packing to accompany her husband on a trip around the world. He was going as a consultant with the Arthur Andersen International Accounting Firm. "George is going on business," she said, "I'm just going along for the fun."

Through the years Lenore has been awarded six honorary degrees from colleges and universities, received citations and honors from more than two dozen associations, and served on many national boards and councils. She was also a commentator on a Detroit radio station for a time.

The Romney family, 1987.
Groupings by families (left to right): Lynn and Larry Kennan family; Jane Robinson family (in center) behind Governor George and Lenore Romney; Mitt and Ann's family (in lightest colors); Scott and Ronna's family (at end right).

In November of 1992, Romney was an active member of the Board of Directors, The Points of Light Foundation, and a member of the Commission on National and Community Service. This calls for speaking engagements across the country and the couple often travel together.

"Until recently I taught spiritual living in Relief Society, an organization of women in our church which I have done for 15 years," Lenore said. And added, looking back:

"Most heartily I have enjoyed working with the National Conference of Christians and Jews as a national campaign chairman: I lectured across the nation for that organization for brotherhood. Also for the Salvation Army, for which they gave me their highest award, the William Booth Statue. I do honor that organization."

Although one might expect their lives to be slightly more relaxed in 1993, it would be foolhardy to assume the Romneys are leading a quiet life. They have 22 grandchildren and 24 great-grandchildren. ❖

❖ Helen W. Milliken ❖

Wife of

Governor William G. Milliken

1969 through 1982

Helen Milliken served a record breaking 14 years as Michigan's First Lady. She started out rather quietly, working behind the scenes as an advocate for the arts and environmental protection. As the years passed, however, she became increasingly involved with women's issues and a nationally recognized vocal proponent in the Equal Rights Amendment struggle.

The second of four children born to a prominent attorney and his wife, Stanley and Nellie Sillik Wallbank, Helen grew up in Denver, Colorado. A slim, attractive girl with naturally curly brown hair and brown eyes, Helen had an inner confidence and quiet dignity. She absorbed her love of gardening from her father. "I always had a garden plot of my own," she recalled.[1]

She attended a private girl's school and went on to Smith College in Northampton, Massachusetts. Between her junior and senior years at Smith she met Staff Sergeant William Grawn Milliken. He had been born in Traverse City on March 26, 1922, and gone to high school there. In 1942, he'd interrupted his studies at Yale University and enlisted in the U.S. Army Air Force. He was stationed at Lowry Field in Colorado, near Denver, when they were introduced by a mutual friend.

"We met. He called. And that was sort of it," Helen recalls. They dated that summer and corresponded after he was sent overseas. While she was completing work on her Bachelor of Arts degree, he was making 50 combat missions as a B-24 waist-gunner in the European Theater of Operations. He was awarded the Air Medal with two Bronze Oak Leaf Clusters, American Campaign Medal, European-African-Middle Eastern Campaign Medal with one Silver Service Star and three Bronze Service Stars, the World War II Victory Medal, and the Purple Heart.[2]

Milliken returned to the United States in May of 1945 and after a series of tentative wedding dates, changed due to conflicting plans with the U.S. Air Force, the couple was married on October 20, in Denver. Following a large church wedding they drove to New Haven, Connecticut, so he could complete his final year at Yale University.

With his degree in hand, the couple planned to leave for Ann Arbor where Milliken had been admitted to the University of Michigan's School of Business Administration for graduate work. His father became ill, however, so they moved to Traverse City to help with the family department store. It had been founded by his grandfather and run by his father until this time.

William G. Milliken
State Archives

The Millikens' first child, William Jr., was born on October 14, 1946, and their daughter, Elaine, was born on June 6, 1948. Helen spent many hours helping in the store during the critical years which followed while her husband rebuilt the department store business. As the children grew older, Helen took part in school and community affairs. She served as president of the local Parent-Teachers Association, president of the Friendly Garden Club, worked in the Red Cross and United Fund, and helped organize the Traverse City League of Women Voters.[3]

The transition from Colorado to Michigan had been natural for Helen with the same opportunities to garden, cook, read, swim, sail, ski, and play tennis. Under Milliken's presidency, J. W. Milliken, Inc. expanded into a small chain. In 1956 they could afford to build a contemporary, four bedroom home with a beautiful view on Grand Traverse Bay.

It appeared their life pattern was established. But Milliken's family had been friends of Governor Chase S. Osborn and Milliken had carried on a correspondence with him while he was in high school. Osborn had encouraged Miliken to enter politics. Milliken's philosophy of going through various phases in life came also to the forefront, "I know when I've reached the end of an era or a period... and it's time to move on to something else."[4] He decided to run for a seat in the Michigan State Senate.

Helen visited the R. E. Olds Museum in Lansing in 1983 to view their exhibit of her inaugural gowns. From left: the inauguration of Governor George Romney when William G. Milliken was lieutenant governor; the inaugural reception honoring President Jimmy Carter, and the inauguration of President Ronald Reagan. Lansing State Journal

"I never expected Bill to be in politics, although his father and grandfather had both served as state senators," Helen recalled. She laid aside her gardening tools, albeit somewhat reluctantly, and pitched in to help with his campaign.

Milliken won the 1960 senate race and was re-elected in 1962. He spent the weeks in Lansing when the legislature was in session, returning most weekends to their Traverse City home, where Helen remained with their two high school age children.

When he was elected lieutenant governor in 1964, however, young Bill and Elaine were in preparatory schools in the East, so Helen moved to Lansing with him.

Her obligations in this role were not overly demanding and she eased them into a schedule so she could enter Michigan State University's School for Landscaping Architecture. But on January 22, 1969, Governor George Romney resigned to become Secretary of Housing and Urban Development in Washington. Four hours later Milliken was governor of Michigan. This time Helen put her gardening books aside.

Bill Jr., Elaine, Lieutenant Governor William Milliken, and Helen on the patio of their home overlooking Grand Traverse Bay, in 1966.

One of her first tasks was moving into the state's newly acquired Governor's Residence. The furniture came with the house, so Helen stored some items to make room for their own favorite pieces and they settled in. She brought in works by Michigan artists to hang on a rotating display. Mary Browder, who had been Lenore Romney's secretary, continued in this role for Helen, and it made the transition easier.

The Millikens entertained frequently and Helen made it a point to show visitors through the first residence provided by the state for a governor. She wanted people to appreciate the understated elegance of the house. Under her guidance the 3.2-acre grounds were renovated and tended to restore the beautiful setting.

Helen at first found public speaking difficult. But she steeled herself and "just did it" because she was dedicated to preserving the environment. She was soon in demand as a public speaker throughout the state. She fought billboards and throw-away bottles with a passion, was an out-spoken advocate for curtailing oil drilling in the Pigeon River State Forest, and publicly voiced her dismay when legislators proposed converting some of the Capitol Building lawn into a parking lot.

Although she'd had virtually no interest in politics, "I discovered it was a whole dimension of life I didn't know anything about," Helen said. She learned quickly, however, and became an experienced campaigner for and adviser to her husband. She also realized that her position as First Lady provided special opportunities and she used them judiciously.

"My beliefs are not particularly unique," she has said. "It's just that I'm now in a position to do something about them and to help in my husband's efforts to achieve a better quality of life for all citizens."

Both Helen and Milliken have a deep appreciation for the arts and she was a leader in the establishment of the Artrain project in 1968. With actual railroad cars containing works of art, the nation's only touring art museum opened its doors in 1971. In March of 1983, the studio car was named "The Helen W. Milliken Studio" in her honor. By that time it had become a familiar sight in cities and villages all through Michigan and had visited more than 200 communities in 23 different states.

During Milliken's last four years as governor, Helen became increasingly interested in women's issues. She emerged from being a participant to a leader in the movement for greater equality and involvement of women in government. In 1977, she was elected a delegate from Michigan to the International Women's Year Conference in Houston, Texas.

In 1979, Helen was named co-chair of ERAmerica along with Sharon Percy Rockefeller. It was an alliance of more than 200 organizations formed to win ratification of the Equal Rights Amendment (ERA). "We are involved with more than women's rights here," she said, "because by guaranteeing the rights of any one segment of our society we build protection for the rights of all."

"I also committed myself to the issue of choice and reproductive rights," she said. After Milliken left office, she continued her work in the ERA and became a member of the national board of the National Abortion Rights Action League (NARAL). Of the latter, she observed, "That is obviously a struggle that has yet to be won."

The term, Touch of Steel, has been used to describe her husband and it also fits Helen. She had breast cancer surgery in October of 1982. Only 19 days after her mastectomy, she headed a Michigan delegation on a previously planned, official trip to China. When she celebrated her 60th birthday, Helen pointed out that if life was all down-hill from now on, that would be a positive thing for her because she is a skier.

When Milliken did not seek re-election after 14 years in office, the couple returned to their Traverse City home. In 1984, they built a cottage on Mackinac Island and spend their weekends there during the summers. Both have carried on with their outside interests. He served as founding chairman of the Center for the Great Lakes, an environmental organization headquartered in Chicago to protect the Great Lakes, served on the board of the Ford Foundation, and remains on several corporate boards of directors.

"In the years since leaving Lansing, I have been fortunate in having opportunities to travel, including the U.N. International Women's Conference in Nairobi in 1985," Helen pointed out in 1992. "I have also traveled to India, Nepal, Indonesia, South Africa, Zimbabwe, Chili, Argentina, and Brazil. All of which have afforded me the opportunity to observe and better understand the plight of Third World women.

"But it is all a matter of degree, for I do think that women are far from equal in this society... economically, politically or socially... with minimum progress over the last decade. And still no ERA!"

Both warm and friendly people, Milliken and Helen continue to keep in touch with friends they made during their 14 years in Lansing. Among these are former Lieutenant Governor, now Supreme Court Justice, James Brickley and his wife, Joyce Braithwaite, who was Milliken's executive assistant. ❖

Paula L. Blanchard

Wife of

Governor James J. Blanchard

1983 to 1987

Paula Parker Blanchard was born in November of 1944, during the World War II years, and grew up in an era when women were broadening their roles in society. She was intelligent, capable and had no qualms about doing what she set out to do.

Some said she was representative of this period in the feminist movement and 30 years of unbridled individualism. Others said she was simply Paula and would have represented herself well in any era.

When her husband was sworn into the Office of Governor in 1983, Paula enthusiastically began fulfilling her role as First Lady and enjoyed the inherent challenges. But she eventually became frustrated by the fact that she had lost control of her personal life and was, in fact, leading the life of her husband's choosing.

A spirited girl, with blue eyes and black hair, pretty Paula Lynne Parker was raised in the Oakland County village of Clarkston. Her parents were both Junior High School teachers and she had one brother, Lawrence, who was five years younger.

During her high school years she was a leader in school government and activities. She entered Michigan State University and obtained her Bachelor of Arts degree in elementary education in 1966. Paula graduated with honors and was named one of the 50 Outstanding Senior Women in her class.

While at the university, she met fellow student James J. Blanchard and they were married a week after her graduation. She taught fourth grade in Richfield, Minnesota, while he completed work on his law degree at the University of Minnesota. In 1968, the couple moved to Lansing and he began working in the state Attorney General's Office. She taught second grade in an elementary school in Lansing until their son, Jay, was born on October 1, 1970.

Four years later, Blanchard was elected to the U.S. Congress and they moved to Washington, D.C. During the next eight years, Paula had a certain anonymity. She was a member of the 94th Congressional Club Wives and other congressional associations. She worked part-time as the administrative assistant to the president of the Animal Health Institute, a private, nonprofit trade association. She also studied for her master's degree in Business Administration at American University.

Although Paula enjoyed the experiences in Washington, she wanted to return to Michigan. She encouraged her husband to run for governor and helped him campaign.

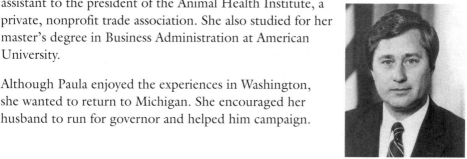

James J. Blanchard
State Archives

137

When Blanchard won the election, Paula made the most of the position as First Lady. She began working in the Michigan Department of Commerce as an unpaid adviser in a full-time position. She established the Office of Michigan Products Promotion and was keenly interested in its success. She was the only governor's wife at the time to have an office in a state department and devote full-time to its programs and activities.[1]

She also started opening the Governor's Summer Residence on Mackinac Island to the public for a free Wednesday morning tour each week during summer months. In addition, she completed the necessary courses for her master's degree in telecommunication at Michigan State University.

Marital problems that had existed in previous years were exacerbated, not resolved, when Blanchard became governor "due to the increasing and consuming demands of public office," she pointed out later.[2] Six months after his re-election in November of 1986,

Paula Blanchard in her Department of Commerce office, 1983.
Willah Weddon

Paula started divorce proceedings. Such an act was unprecedented in the history of Michigan's Governors, but the arrangements were conducted quietly and in a dignified, friendly manner.

Paula entered the business world as associate vice president of a large public relations firm in the Detroit area. By 1990, she had written a book, *Til Politics Do Us Part*, which was published a few months before the next gubernatorial election and chronicled her years in public life.

In 1991, she was promoted to vice president in the firm she was employed by and was named by *Crain's Detroit Business Magazine* as one of 15 most successful women executives in Detroit. In 1993, Paula became vice president, communications, of the National Fund for U.S. Botanical Gardens in Washington, D.C. ❖

❖ Janet A. Blanchard ❖

Wife of

Governor James J. Blanchard

1989 - 1990

anet A. Blanchard was Michigan's First Lady for 16 months, from September 2, 1989, until January 1, 1991, during Governor James Blanchard's second and last term in office.

The couple was married on September 2, 1989, in a private ceremony with about 100 guests at the Michigan Governor's Summer Residence on Mackinac Island. Janet was 38 years old and Blanchard was 46 years old at the time of their wedding. The marriage was the second for both. He had been divorced two years previously from Paula Blanchard and had one son, Jay, who had entered Michigan State University while his father was governor.

Lansing State Journal

Janet was born to Alice and Howard Eifert on October 25, 1950, and grew up on a farm near Mason, about 12 miles from Lansing. She was active in 4H work as a girl, raising and showing Angus cattle. She and her brother, Thomas, who was four years older, enjoyed farm life and Janet never forgot the role women play in Michigan's agricultural economy.[1]

After graduating from high school, Janet attended Western Michigan University (WMU) and began a 20-year career in public service. During this time she was married, but divorced after nine years. Determined to complete her education, she took courses on a part-time basis until she received a Bachelor of Arts degree from WMU in liberal arts in December of 1988.

Her years of public service included working in various management and administrative positions for Michigan's Departments of Education, Commerce, Civil Service, Labor, and Management and Budget.

"I never knew Jim Blanchard when he was in Congress," she pointed out.[2] But she joined the Governor's staff in 1983 and helped establish the new administration's personnel operations and oversaw executive appointments for several state departments.

From 1987 to 1990, Janet served as deputy director of the Governor's Cabinet Council on Human Investment. The council was "kind of an innovative office," as she described it, that concentrated on ways to improve the caliber of the state's work force. She also co-chaired and directed the Governor's Telecommunication Task Force from 1988 to 1990. The task force was responsible for developing recommendations and a long-term plan for building a state telecommunications network of the future.

Janet continued her work in these positions for six months after her marriage before she took a leave of absence. Then she became a strong advocate for the Neighborhood Builders Alliance, which provides grants to improve the quality, safety and economic stability of local neighborhoods. She visited more than 60 counties and hundreds of communities, schools, and businesses throughout the state to build local support and participation in the Alliance.

Despite their joint efforts, Blanchard narrowly lost the election in November and in January of 1991, Michigan had a new First Lady.

Disappointed not to be able to embark on a third term and follow through with their plans, Janet and Blanchard entered the world of private enterprise. Although they maintained a residence in Beverly Hills, Michigan, he became a partner in a Washington, D.C. law firm. Politics were not forgotten, however. They were both active in supporting the successful Presidential nominee, William Clinton, during the Democratic party's 1992 Convention in New York.[3]

The couple continued their work on into the Presidential campaign and when Clinton won the election, Blanchard's name was mentioned prominently for a cabinet position. But it was Janet who first joined the new administration. She became deputy personnel director for the White House.

Things changed on May 27, 1993, when President Clinton nominated Blanchard to serve as U.S. Ambassador to Canada. Janet quit her job in the White House and they both began studying French in preparation for the assignment in Ottawa, Canada. The couple moved to Ottawa, but have kept their suburban Detroit residence. ❖

James J. Blanchard
State Archives

❖ Michelle D. Engler ❖

Wife of

Governor John M. Engler

1991-

Michelle DeMunbrun Engler, a native Texan, had met John M. Engler in 1989, but they became acquainted while they were visiting mutual friends in the spring of 1990, in Florida. A former state senator, Engler was in the midst of a heated political campaign for the Governor's seat in Michigan. Their romance flourished during the following months, but their engagement was not announced until after he won the election in November. He saw no reason to subject her to the rigors of the campaign and the announcement came as a surprise to nearly everyone.

The couple, both lawyers and both Catholics, were married on December 8, 1990, in the bride's hometown of San Antonio, Texas. Less than a month later, Michelle became Michigan's First Lady when Engler was sworn into the Office of Governor on January 1, 1991.

Engler, born October 12, 1948, had served in the Michigan House of Representatives from 1970 until elected to the state senate in 1978, where he'd served as majority leader until he decided to run for governor in 1990.

Since the 1930s, virtually all First Ladies had played a role in their husband's campaigns and, as a result, most had gained some practical political experience.

Being a newcomer to both Michigan and politics, blonde Michelle faced an immediate challenge. She was surprised at some of the strong partisan feelings, but her background had prepared her exceptionally well for her new role. In addition to her education as a lawyer, the first governor's wife to hold such a degree, she has an out-going personality. Her optimistic outlook on life and keen sense of humor are also invaluable assets.

Born in San Antonio on March 24, 1958, Michelle was the second of Richard and Margaret DeMunbrun's four children. Her father is an architect and her mother works for a church. Michelle's older brother, Richard Jr., and two younger sisters, Stephanie and Renee, are pursuing their own professional careers in Texas.[1]

An avid reader from the time she was a young girl, Michelle always wanted to be a lawyer. An active youngster, she grew up enjoying swimming, watersports, softball, and volleyball. She is fond of country and western music, enjoys musicals, barbeques, and is an enthusiastic fan of professional basketball.

Entering the University of Texas, Michelle completed her undergraduate work with a major in government. She continued her studies there until she received her law degree. At the time of her marriage, she was a partner in a prestigious Houston law firm specializing in Federal bankruptcy laws.

Although both had been married before, many of the Governor's friends have pointed out that Michelle is "the best thing that ever happened to John Engler." To which, she quickly responds, "He is the best thing that ever happened to me." They have formed a working relationship based on love and a deep respect for the other's abilities and opinions.

Starting married life in the Governor's Residence was considerably different from that of most brides. Michelle put some family pictures on one of the tables in the living room, including one of young John on the family farm, where he was raised near Mt. Pleasant. Outside of this, there were few changes she could make in a house already furnished and owned by the state of Michigan.

Within a few short months after becoming First Lady, Michelle was immersed in the state's literacy programs and helping young children. "I really enjoy meeting and working with people. I love the fact that schoolchildren invite me to come and read to them," she explained. "I find working with literacy programs and volunteerism very fulfilling because both are so fundamental to addressing many social problems we face as a society."

She also began working with former Governor George Romney in the Michigan Volunteer Coalition. "The goal of the coalition is to promote the creation of new voluntary action centers and to raise the visibility and strengthen the existing centers. Studies show that a lot of people don't volunteer because they don't realize what opportunities are out there," she said. "As First Lady I can raise people's awareness and promote the numerous and worthwhile ways in which people can... through their volunteer efforts... help others and make this world a better place to live."

By the end of her first year as First Lady, her husband had appointed Michelle to head a newly-created Michigan Community Service Commission. Designed to lend a hand to community groups, it was part of the Department of Labor which actively pursued assistance to communities that wanted to help themselves in various projects.

Engler had long been a supporter of President George Bush, heading his 1988 campaign in Michigan, and Michelle joined wholeheartedly in the 1992 campaign. The couple traveled extensively throughout the state with the President and Barbara Bush during his unsuccessful bid for re-election in the fall.

In the spring of 1993, Michelle decided she could return to her personal career and still continue her activities as

John M. Engler
State Archives

First Lady. She was sworn in as a member of the State Bar of Michigan and joined a Grand Rapids-based law firm on a part-time basis, starting April 1.

"I have come to feel at home here in Michigan," Michelle says with a smile. She enjoys the beauty of changing seasons and especially appreciates the snow. As for the people in her adopted state, they have found Michelle an open, friendly, articulate and intelligent woman. ❖

Michelle Engler in the Governor's Residence.   Willah Weddon

❖ Michigan's ❖
Women
Lieutenant Governors

❖ Matilda Dodge Wilson ❖

Lieutenant Governor

November 1940 - January 1941

Matilda Rausch Dodge Wilson became the state's first woman to serve as lieutenant governor on November 19, 1940, when she was appointed to the office by Governor Luren Dickinson.

Dickinson, who had been lieutenant governor, was sworn into office on March 17, 1939, the day after the death of Governor Frank D. Fitzgerald. This left the office of lieutenant governor vacant. It remained vacant until Dickinson's appointment of Matilda Wilson, 20 months later. She held the office six weeks, until newly elected Governor Murray Van Wagoner and his lieutenant governor took office.

Dickinson had long been a supporter of woman suffrage and felt women were capable of holding public office. Although he said he made the appointment to test the state laws of succession, he could have appointed her when the vacancy first occurred. He must have been aware of the ruckus it would cause, however, and delayed until he'd lost his bid for re-election before making the appointment.

He had guessed right. Opposition for even this short period was heated. Attorney General Thomas Read said, "The laws of succession are clear. Should Governor Dickinson now die or become incapacitated, we would be in a fine mess.

"Had he not appointed Mrs. Wilson, Harry F. Kelly, as secretary of state, would have become the governor, and he is a man well qualified. Now what have we?" he asked.[2] He added that he meant no disrespect and considered Wilson to be a "fine woman." (Read, himself, had served as lieutenant governor from 1921 to 1924 and 1935 to 1936.)

Matilda handled it well. "I will carry out whatever duties devolve upon me from my apppointment," she said. "I feel it is a symbol of Governor Dickinsons's belief in the place of women in public, not a compliment to me, but to the women of Michigan."[3]

She attended a regular meeting of the state administration board. Then, on January 1, 1941, Governor Van Wagoner took office and her term was ended.

Matilda was an excellent choice for the office and would have performed well in this capacity for the full period. It should be noted that this woman could have bought and sold the men who were most vocal in their opposition to her appointment. She had, in fact, played a significant role in accumulating the family fortune and managed her inheritance and the children's trust funds for years. She probably had more people working for her than the Attorney General at that time.

Matilda was also well versed in politics. She attended the 1928 Republican National Convention as one of ten women in the 66 member Michigan Delegation. She was treasurer of the National Council of Women, an organization working for women's rights and the advancement of women, and was a delegate from the council to an international meeting in Vienna, Austria, in May of 1930. She was elected to the state Board of Agriculture in 1931 and went to the meetings in Lansing.[1]

Matilda Rausch was born on October 19, 1883, to George and Margaret Rausch, in Walkerton, Ontario. The next year her parents moved to Detroit where her sister, Amelia, was born in 1887. Their father ran a bar in downtown Detroit and their mother kept a boarding house next door.[2]

Matilda entered Gorsline Business College, learned secretarial skills, and in 1902 began working for John and Horace Dodge. Their engineering business was just beginning to be successful and Matilda contributed to its growth. She and John were married in 1907 and she became a U.S. citizen. After their wedding, she met his children by his first wife who had died in 1902. They were Winifred, age 14; Isabel, age 12; and John Duval, age 9.

As the Dodge brothers' business grew into the fourth largest automobile producer in the United States, Matilda and John had three children of their own: Frances, born in 1914; Daniel, in 1917; and Anna Margaret, in 1919. During this time, Matilda not only contributed large amounts of money, but spent hours working for the First Presbyterian Church, the Salvation Army, and the Red Cross.

In 1920, John Dodge died unexpectedly of influenza during a trip to New York, and Anna, not quite 5 years old, died in 1924 from complications following the measles. Matilda spent more than a year abroad where she absorbed European culture.

On June 29, 1925, Matilda married her second husband, Alfred E. Wilson, a wealthy lumberman. The couple had known each other a long time and were both active in the Presbyterian Church. They adopted two children, Richard and Barbara, in 1930.

Tragedy struck again when her son, Daniel Dodge, died in an accident at the age of 21, while on his honeymoon on Manitoulin Island. Always experimenting, he had apparently lighted a stick of old dynamite that exploded before he could throw it away. His bride of two weeks, two wounded men and the wife of one of them, tried to get Dan to the hospital on the mainland in his speed boat. They said he stood up and fell overboard.

Dan's body was not found until more than three weeks later by fishermen. The impact on Matilda was devastating and those close to her said she was never the same again. He was the only male heir to the Dodge estate and Matilda had this in mind when she'd built the magnificent mansion, Meadow Brook Hall.

Described at various times as spunky, determined, well-organized, and strong-minded, Matilda was also known for her lively sense of humor. She enjoyed bridge, horseback riding, and dancing. To the last day of her life she was interested in raising and showing her harness show ponies and six-horse hitch of matched Belgian horses.

In 1956, the Wilsons arranged with Dr. John A. Hannah, President of Michigan State University, to donate their 1,600 acre estate and a $2 million building fund, to create M.S.U.-Oakland, which later became Oakland University. They retained Meadow Brook Hall, another house, and 127 acres for their use until they died.

Matilda had received an honorary degree from Michigan State University in 1955, and in 1960 she was named to the Michigan Cultural Commission by the Governor.

Alfred Wilson died from a heart attack in Scottsdale, Arizona, on April 6, 1962. Matilda returned to Meadow Brook Hall with the newly created university nearby. She enjoyed the students so much that she was soon having the time of her life. She continued her active participation in many organizations, and she was especially pleased when she was presented with the first William Booth Award by the Salvation Army in 1965.

At the age of 83, Matilda went to Belgium to purchase a team of Belgian horses, but suffered a massive heart attack while there and died on September 19, 1967. Her body was brought home, services were held in the First Presbyterian Church, and her body was placed in the Wilson Mausoleum.

Matilda left a $16.1 million estate, about $15 million of it in the Matilda R. Wilson Fund, a charitable trust. Although her daughter, Frances, and the two Wilson children tried to dissolve the trust, a probate judge ruled that Matilda's will represented the pattern of her life and was to remain intact. By 1971, the estate was settled and Oakland University received Meadow Brook Hall and the adjoining land. ❖

Lansing State Journal

❖ Martha W. Griffiths ❖

Lieutenant Governor

1983 through 1990

Martha Griffiths, the first woman to be elected lieutenant governor of Michigan, broke many records and set new ones during her 42 years of public service. She fought all her political life for women's and civil rights and went out of office fighting age discrimination.

One of the chief duties of lieutenant governor is to preside over the senate and 78 year-old Martha took her job seriously. Frail and sometimes accused of being forgetful, she could be heard gaveling senators down with, "Be quiet or I'll put you out of here."[1] And while the senators complained that she treated them like children, statehouse pundits retorted that it may have been because they acted like children.

There was no question about Martha being the party matriarch, however, and when Governor James J. Blanchard dropped her for a younger running mate in his 1990 bid for a third term, the fur began to fly. Despite Blanchard's denial that age was a factor, Martha took issue with him publicly. When party members urged her to be quiet for party unity, she replied that women had been quiet too long and continued to voice her displeasure. This time the issue was ageism.

Lansing political analyist William Ballenger III, predicted that if it was a very close election, dumping Martha might make the difference between Blanchard's winning or losing.[2] He lost by a narrow margin.

Martha was born on January 29, 1912, in Pierce City, Missouri. She wanted to be a journalist and received her bachelor's degree from the University of Missouri. But after graduation she became enchanted by law and entered the University of Michigan law school.[3] She married Hicks G. Griffiths, and in 1940 they were the first married couple to graduate from the university's law school.[4]

In 1946, Martha and Hicks opened the law firm of Griffiths, Griffiths, and Schon in Detroit. They were keenly interested in politics and in 1948 they met with G. Mennen Williams and several other Democrats in the basement of their home. Plans were laid to overthrow ineffective Democratic leadership and they campaigned hard. That fall Martha was elected to the State House of Representatives (1949-52) and Williams elected governor of Michigan (1949-1960).

She made an unsuccessful bid for a seat in the U.S. House of Representatives in 1952, but was undaunted by defeat and made plans to run again in two years. Meanwhile, she was appointed the first woman judge and recorder of Detroit's Recorders Court (1953). Her campaign for a congressional seat was a close one, but she turned the tables on the candidate who'd defeated her previously and won the election in 1954. Her margins increased in each election as she held her post in Washington for the next 20 years.

Martha hadn't planned to make women's rights her cause. "I didn't approve of bra-burning and screaming and marching and all that silly stuff," she explained. But as legislation crossed her desk, she became aware that on almost every page they were discriminating against women.[5]

She is credited with adding the word "sex" to the 1964 Civil Rights Act, thus including women in the legislation aimed at banning discimination, and getting House members to approve it. In the late 1960s she served as a member of the Ways and Means and Joint Economic Committees. In the latter capacity she conducted a series of hearings on the economic position of women.

Martha gained her greatest victory when she shepherded the Equal Rights Amendment through the House of Representatives in 1971. She returned to Michigan to make sure the amendment was approved by the state legislature and then she served on the national committee working for its ratification.

By 1974, Martha decided she'd quit politics, leave Washington, and spend time with her husband and her law practice. Back home, she accepted corporate board positions with Chrysler, Consumers Power, Burroughs, K-mart, Greyhound, Xerox, the National Bank of Detroit, Ford Hospital, Mercy College of Detroit, and the American Automobile Association of Michigan.

Then along came James Blanchard, 1981 Democrat contender for the governorship, with an invitation to join him on the ticket as lieutenant governor. Martha accepted, and in November of 1982, became the first woman elected to hold the position. From 1982 through 1990, she carried out her duties. She examined state contracts and bidding procedures for the Governor, presided over the senate and helped out in the next political campaign.

By 1990, she was 78 years-old and had spent 42 years in political life. It was expected that she would announce her retirement from the $80,300-a-year post because of her husband's failing health. In a surprise move she announced in May, "If the Governor and the Democratic convention think I am qualified to run, I will run. I have experience, I am qualified, and I am available."[6]

The Governor hedged and finally, in August, announced that he wanted another running mate... one who would "be ready at a moment's notice to step in and take over the heavy responsiblity of being governor should anything unforeseen happen to me."[7]

Martha had no intention of bowing out gracefully, saying discimination against age was involved here. She refused to attend a tribute planned for her during the Democrat convention. Later, she said she wanted to be remembered for having helped a large percentage of the population, not just for women, but for blacks and Latinos... for all the people.

Although retired, in the 1992 election Martha endorsed a state-wide candidate she had known a long time and felt was the best qualified. He just happened to be a Republican. ❖

❖ Connie B. Binsfeld ❖

Lieutenant Governor

1991 -

When Connie Binsfeld was named Michigan's 1977 Mother of the Year, she was in her second term as a state representative. Governor William Milliken said at the time: "Bringing up five children may have developed the intuitiveness, diplomacy, and good judgement that has earned her the respect and admiration of her colleagues in the House of Representatives where she serves with skill and dedication. She is a warm and friendly person, whose concern for others is reflected in personal service to her community."

His assessment of Connie was equally appropriate when she was elected lieutenant governor on the ticket with John Engler 1990. She had served her constituents and the state well during the preceding 16 years she'd spent in Lansing. Far from being spectacular, she'd followed a steady course which she continued in her new position as presiding officer of the senate.

Where her predecessor, Martha Griffiths, had banged the gavel to hush a sometimes unruly senate, "Connie uses the silent approach to it," said Senator Harry Gast of St. Joseph. "She'll tap her gavel gently and slow and they know they've got to shape up."[1]

Connie Berube Binsfeld was born on April 18, 1924, in the Upper Peninsula city of Munising. Her mother, a teacher, was widowed and left with three children to raise. Connie never forgot how her mother had to leave her first teaching job because her contract said she forfeited her job if she married. And, after her husband died, she returned to teaching, but her pay was less than the male teachers' because "they had a family to support."[2]

After graduating from high school in Munising, where her mother taught for 40 years, Connie received her B.S. degree in secondary education from Siena Heights College in Adrian, and later did post-graduate work in political science at Wayne State University. She began her career as a teacher in Pontiac, and, in 1947, married John Binsfeld of Grosse Pointe Woods, a consulting engineer. They lived in the Oakland County area for 20 years and had five children: John, Gregory, Susan, Paul, and Michael.

The Binsfelds moved to Glen Lake, where they had summered for years, in 1968. Here Connie was a volunteer in the hospital, scouting, and the Parent Teacher's Association. She was a member of the Glen Lake Women's Club, the Grand Traverse Area Women's Political Caucus, the St. Rita-St. Joseph Church in Maple City, and the Leelanau County Republican Committee.

With the Binsfeld children all in school, Connie decided to get more involved in the local political scene and to "help make democracy work at the grass roots level." In 1970, she entered the race for a seat on the Leelanau County Commission, won the election, and served two terms.

In 1974, she "hung up her apron," as she described the move with her quiet, understated sense of humor. With the support of her family, she ran a successful campaign for a seat in the Michigan House of Representatives.[3] She served four terms, from 1974 to 1982 in the House and served on many committees. During her second term she was appointed chairman of a task force on legislative reform. Her goal was to increase efficiency and cut costs in the legislature. She also wanted to make the entire legislative process understandable to Michigan citizens.

In 1979 and 1981, Connie was elected Assistant Republican Leader of the House. Although aptly described as a team player, Connie did not pull her punches when she was convinced something was wrong. In a December 4, 1979 press release, she stated: "In a single action, the House Judiciary Committee, led by a closeminded chairman, has reported a bill that will lead to the degradation and destruction of the family unit in our state." She filled two pages with reasons the bill was so bad and pointed out how the bill she had introduced was better.

Connie was elected to her first term in the state senate in 1982 and served two consecutive four-year terms. During her first year in the senate, she was elected Assistant Majority Leader. She also served on a number of important committees and was the first woman ever appointed to the Capital Outlay Subcommittee on Appropriations. She gained national recognition for being the prime sponsor of the Michigan Surrogacy Act which prohibits commerical surrogacy in this state.

Of the 41 bills she had passed into laws, she cites three as her best-known accomplishments: a 1977 domestic violence package, the environmental bonding issue approved by Michigan voters, and the ban on surrogate mothering for money.

President Ronald Reagan appointed her to the North Country Scenic Trail Council in 1983 and she enjoyed this work. It coincided with her love of cross-country skiing in the woods surrounding her home and canoeing on Glen Lake and down the Crystal River. Later, she was appointed to the National Park Advisory Board by the President George Bush administration.

Although Connie had been one of three finalists in contention for lieutenant governor in the 1986 gubernatorial campaign, she lost out. In 1990, however, John Engler picked her as his running mate. They had worked together in the senate when he was majority leader, and their philosophies meshed. They had differences, but Connie was never hesitant to point out her convictions, and they respected each other's opinions.

There had been some suggestions that, if Engler was elected, Connie would become a department director. When in office, however, she said, "I opted to make my presiding over the senate a very important role. And I told the Governor I wanted to focus on children's issues." Her singleness of purpose was again apparent.

The newly-elected Governor appointed her to chair a 12-person commission to study adoption and the Binsfeld Commission on Adoption presented its recommendations to Governor Engler in April of 1992. "Most of those recommendations are now being implemented," she pointed out that fall.

Although it's unlikely any lieutenant governor could cause great changes, Connie Binsfeld has been applauded for doing what she does well and in depth. ❖

❖ Governor's Official Residences: ❖ Lansing and Mackinac Island

lthough there was no official Governor's Residence in Lansing until 1969, Michigan's Governors and their families had enjoyed a summer residence on Mackinac Island since 1945. Prior to that time they had been able to spend many summers on the island in temporary quarters provided by the Michigan Park Service.

During the years Michigan was a territory and for the first years of statehood, Detroit was the capital city. This posed no housing problem for the families of governors since they already lived in Detroit. Elizabeth Cass, Emily Mason (sister and hostess for Stevens T. Mason), Julia Mason, and Juliana Woodbridge continued living in their own homes while their husbands served as governors. Their private homes automatically served as the Governor's place for government business and social functions.

As the population fanned out from the Detroit area, governors were elected from Constantine, Marshall, Ann Arbor, and Adrian. This meant that Mary Gordon, Mary Barry, Lucretia Felch, and Elizabeth Greenly spent many days alone while their husbands were in Detroit. If they made the trip, however, they could get accommodations in the city.

Governor's Residence in Lansing. Willah Weddon

When Lansing was approved as the site of the new capital in March of 1847, it consisted of a sawmill and a few log buildings. The area was a dense forest on the banks of the Grand River, virtually nothing but trees and swamps. A temporary Capitol Building was erected and Epaphroditus Ransom was inaugurated there in 1848.

Scene at rear of Governor's Residence soon after it was acquired by the state. Willah Weddon

A house in Lansing was said to have been built during the time Ransom was governor to serve as the Governor's Mansion. But when incoming Governor Barry saw it, he reportedly said it was too small for an Executive Mansion and refused to live in it. It became the home of a lieutenant governor and later housed several state officials. If the house, on the corner of Allegan Street and Capitol Avenue, was intended to be the Governor's Residence, it was never used as such.

This city in the wilderness was much less accessible than Detroit and governors' families visited only on rare occasions. It was a hard trip on rough or muddy roads under the best of conditions.

Ironically, although the women found travel to Lansing difficult, they made trips to Washington, D.C. with their husbands. Mary Bingham, for instance, stayed in South Lyon while Kinsley Bingham was in Lansing, but made a visit with him for several months to the nation's capital when he was in Congress.

Conditions in Lansing improved through the years and by the time Governor John Bagley took office in 1873, he resided there during the legislative sessions and Frances was on hand for state ceremonies. Five years later, the permanent Capitol Building was completed in time for the inauguration of Governor Charles Croswell and Elizabeth joined him for his second inauguration.

The first family to make Lansing their permanent home during his term of office was that of Russell and Annette Alger with their six children. From then on it appears to have been a matter of preference whether the families moved to Lansing or stayed in their hometowns. Lucretia Rich, with no children, lived in a hotel with her husband. Others, such as Mary Sleeper, made trips by train for special events and stayed at the Downey Hotel for as many days as necessary.

For First Families with young children, however, finding living quarters was a problem. Some rented homes and others bought homes. Anne Kelly, Nancy Williams, and Alice Swainson all discovered that finding a place for their families to live was one of their priorities when they became a First Lady.

Official Residence in Lansing

It wasn't until 1969 that an official residence was provided in Lansing for the Governor and his family. Howard Sober, a wealthy trucking executive, and his wife, Letha, had built a home in 1959, in the southwest area of Lansing. By the time they offered to donate it to the state, the market value of the house was estimated at $440,000. Along with the donation, they included a provision that the state pay $250,000 for the furnishings which, they pointed out, had been acquired as an integral part of the architecture during construction.

Located on a 3.2-acre lot, the one-story, 10-room ranch-type house is deceptively compact due to the L-shaped plan. There are other, larger homes in the fashionable neighborhood which appear more mansion-like than this one on Oxford Road. After some haggling by the legislature, the donation was accepted and eventually $210,000 was paid for the furnishings.

Governor William and Helen Milliken were the first to live in the new quarters. They enclosed the screened terrace at the rear with large glass panes to provide extra space for conferences.

During the Blanchard administration, a group called "Friends of the Governor's Residence," raised funds from private sources to redecorate the house and improve the kitchen. The latter allowed the staff to prepare food for large gatherings rather than having food catered.

Michelle and John Engler haven't made any changes in the house. Thus, despite minor improvements made through the years, the basic design remains the same.[1]

Although the house is ideal for entertaining 100 to 150 legislators, it doesn't provide a very comfortable living situation for families. The living room and public areas of the house are in the middle, separating the First Family's bedrooms from the dining room and kitchen. This requires one to walk past the front door, in full view of the living room, to reach the kitchen. As Paula Blanchard observed, she always felt she had to be fully dressed before walking from one end of her house to the other.[2]

The state provides funds to pay for a maid, a handyman and a secretary for the Governor's wife, plus utilities, telephone and routine maintenance.[3] Any major maintenance, such as painting, is done by contract under the supervision of the Department of Management and Budget.

Mackinac Island Summer Home

From the time General Lewis Cass, Territorial Governor, visited Mackinac Island in 1820, Michigan's Governors have appreciated its invigorating climate and beautiful scenery. The coastline around the island is nine miles long and there is a magnificent view of the Straits from the bluffs.

A National Park was established on about half the area in 1875, when Congress designated parts of Mackinac Island to be set aside for the "health, comfort, pleasure, benefit, and enjoyment of the people." In 1895, after the park area had been transferred to Michigan, it became Mackinac Island State Park and a commission was created to administer the nearly 1,800 acres with its historic buildings.

Governor's Summer Residence on Mackinac Island.   Mackinac State Historic Parks

There were several residences built in the 1870s for the officers in Old Fort Mackinac. These were maintained by the park service and in 1888, Governor Cyrus and Mary Luce were the first to spend the entire summer on Mackinac Island. After that, some of the governors' families visited the island occasionally and Governor Fred Green hosted a July 1929, National Governors' Conference there in the famed Grand Hotel.

As more and more time was spent by governors' families summering on the island, it became known as Michigan's Summer Capital. Clara Brucker spent a month in one of the old homes with the Brucker's, 4 year-old son, Wilber Jr., in 1931.

In 1935, the Michigan Legislature authorized a home to be set aside for the Governor during the summer months and appropriated $500 for its operation. The Park Commission designated the former Post Commandant's house for the Governor's exclusive use.[4]

With a Governors' Conference scheduled on the island during July of 1945, the Commission managed to get an appropriation from the legislature to purchase the Scherer house which was on land adjacent to the State Park. It had been built for $15,000 in the fall and winter of 1901 and 1902, by the Lawrence Young family of Chicago and sold to Clara Scherer of Detroit in 1926. During the subsequent years the house had been left to deteriorate and the commission was able to buy it for $15,000, the cost of the original building.

The 24-room, three-story house was built with all-wood interior walls and ceilings, and native white pine was used for framing and exterior shingles. The result was an impressive example of wood architecture. The long porch, perched on a bluff, was built so visitors could relax and gaze out over the Straits of Mackinac.

In the rush to repair the residence for the 37th Annual Governors' Conference, held in July, a number of inmates from the state prison were pressed into service inside and outside the dwelling. Anne Kelly worked alongside the inmates, sewing curtains, and finished just in time to host a luncheon for the wives of the other Governors on July 3, 1945. This launched the cottage, as it has been called by some of the First Ladies, into its future role as a site for many important national and state conferences.

Each summer, Boy Scout troops have traditionally raised and lowered the flag daily at the residence but at the urging of Helen Milliken, Girl Scouts are now occasionally used.[5] When the Governor is in residence, the Michigan flag is flown.

Paula Blanchard introduced a Wednesday morning tour of the residence for visitors to the island. The weekly quota of tickets was always gone, she noted with pleasure. During the open house mornings, she said she usually went off and played tennis.[6] Michelle Engler has continued the Wednesday morning tours for the public.

Although some governors and their families have used the summer residence quite extensively, others haven't used it at all. The State Commission maintains the house and keeps it in readiness for the Governor. A carriage with a team of horses and a driver were provided for the First Family's use, because there are no motor vehicles allowed on the island. This was discontinued by 1981, however, due to the expense.

There is an attraction to the island that continues long after executive terms have ended. Governor Williams and Nancy had a home of their own there after he left office and he is buried on the island.

The Millikens, too, enjoyed the island so much that they built a cottage on it in 1984 and commute during the summer on weekends from their Traverse City home.

Governor Engler has conferences on the island occasionally and Michelle likes it there so much that she tries to stay on a little longer, if she can arrange it in her schedule.[7] ❖

❖ Bibliography ❖

Because a First Lady in Michigan acquires the title by virtue of being married to the sitting Governor, historical research has to begin with him. A First Lady loses her title when her husband leaves office, incidentally, but a governor carries the title when he is addressed for his lifetime.

To determine who was the First Lady during each gubernatorial term, it was important to know which woman the Governor was married to at the time he held office. Several Michigan Governors had two or three wives and this has complicated the search. Only one, so far, has provided the state with two First Ladies during his tenure as governor.

The *Michigan Manual* provides basic information on the governors. It has been published every two years by various state agencies since 1835, and is currently published by the Department of Management and Budget. The Manual contains a brief biography of each governor and usually mentions the fact that he has or had a wife or a family. The complete series of manuals used for research on *First Ladies of Michigan* is located in the State Library of Michigan.

More details about early governors are contained in publications by the Chapman Brothers, Chicago, Illinois. Titles of these changed from county to county, with the inclusion of special information about each county. The same overall material, however, was used in each county edition. A frequently used reference in this text was the *Portrait and Biographical Album of Jackson County Michigan,* which was published by Chapman Brothers in 1890. These descriptions occasionally included something about the First Ladies.

Another source of information about the governors is the *Michigan Pioneer Collection,* which later became the *Michigan History Magazine.*

Claudius B. Grant, the son-in-law of Governor Alpheus Felch, compiled information for the *Governors of the Territory and State of Michigan.* This was edited by George N. Fuller and published as Bulletin Number 16, by the Michigan Historical Commission, Lansing, in 1928.

Other sources used in research for *First Ladies of Michigan* include:

Burke A. Hinsdale, LL.D, edited by Isaac Demmon, *History of the University of Michigan and Biographical Sketches of Regents and Members of the University Senate,* Published by the University of Michigan, Ann Arbor, in 1906. Michigan Historical Collections, Bentley Historical Library, University of Michigan.

F. Clever Bald, *Michigan in Four Centuries,* Harper & Brothers, New York, 1961.

Willis F. Dunbar, *Michigan Through the Centuries*, and, *Michigan: A History of the Wolverine State,* Revised edition edited by George S. May, William Eerdmans Publishing Company, Grand Rapids, Michigan, 1980.

George Weeks, *Stewards of the State: The Governors of Michigan,* by *The Detroit News* and the Historical Society of Michigan, 1991, Revised Second Edition.

Less frequently used sources are credited in the Endnotes and Acknowledgements.

John C. Curry, State Archives of Michigan.

❖ Endnotes and Acknowledgments ❖

ELIZABETH SPENCER CASS   1813 to 1830
1. Willard Baird, *This is Our Michigan,* Federated Publications, Inc., 1959, p.7.
2. Mrs. A. John Kirsch, Detroit, DAR news release, September 17, 1976.
3. *Michigan Biographies,* Michigan Historical Commission, Lansing, 1924, p.156.
4. Frank B. Woodford, *Cass,* Rutgers University Press.
5. Henry Ledyard, Grosse Pointe Farms, in letters to the author, 1992.
6. Mrs. M. R. Putnam, *Grosse Pointe News,* September 17, 1976.
Also see: Silas Farmer, *History of Detroit; Detroit Free Press,* June 3, 1951, Section D; *Burton Historical Collection,* Detroit Public Library; *Cass Papers,* William L. Clements Library, University of Michigan, Ann Arbor.
Special thanks to the Elizabeth Cass Chapter, Daughters of the American Revolution, Grosse Pointe Farms; the late Mrs. Myron J. Dikeman, Detroit; Avis Kirsch, Detroit; and Henry Ledyard, (descendant) Grosse Pointe Farms, Michigan.

EMILY VIRGINIA MASON (Sister)   1831 into 1838
1. George Weeks, *Stewards of the State: The Governors of Michigan,* The Detroit News and the Historical Society of Michigan, 1991, Revised Second Edition. p.14.
2. Jean Frazier, *Michigan History Magazine,* January/February issue 1980, p.30.
3. Lawton T. Hemans, *Life and Times of Stevens Thomson Mason, The Boy Governor of Michigan,* Michigan Historical Commission, Lansing, 1920, p.101.
4. Ibid., p.154.
5. Ibid., p.154.
6. Jean M. Fox, "I Went to the People..." *Fred M. Warner: Progressive Governor,* Farmington Hills Historical Commission, 1988, p.133-34.
7. *Detroit Free Press, Detroit News,* June 4, 1905.
8. *Detroit News and Tribune,* June 1, 1908.
9. Elmwood Cemetery, Detroit, Joe Malburg, October 1992.
Special thanks to John Curry, State Archives, Nov. 13, 1992.

JULIA PHELPS MASON   1838 through 1839
1. Jean Frazier, correspondence, August 1977.
2. Lawton T. Hemans, *Life and Times of Stevens Thomson Mason, The Boy Governor of Michigan,* Michigan Historical Commission, Lansing, 1920, p.452.
3. Ibid., p.452.
4. *Lansing State Journal,* 1955
Also see: *Michigan History Magazine,* Michigan Historical Commission, Spring 1931, p.368; *Portrait and Biographical Album of Jackson County Michigan,* May 1890; *Associated Press,* August 16, 1978, as published in the *Lansing State Journal,* p.B10.

JULIANA TRUMBULL WOODBRIDGE   1840 into 1841
1. *Portrait and Biographical Album of Jackson County Michigan,* Chapman Brothers, Chicago, Illinois, May 1890.

2. Emily George R.S.M., *William Woodbridge, Michigan's Connecticut Yankee,* Michigan History Divison, Michigan Department of State, Lansing 1979, p.8.
3. Ibid., p.18.
4. Jean Frazier, Lansing, in a statement to the author, August 1977.
5. *Portrait and Biographical Album of Jackson County Michigan,* Chapman Brothers, Chicago, Illinois, May 1890.

Also see: Woodbridge clippings, Michigan State Library, Lansing; *History of the University of Michigan with Biographical Sketches of Regents and Members of the University Senate,* 1906, p.166; Christi M. Barnes, *The National Portrait Gallery,* November 28, 1992.

Special thanks to David M. Edgar, Easton, Pennsylvania, August 1993.

MARY HUDUN GORDON   1841

1. George Weeks, *Stewards of the State: The Governors of Michigan,* The Detroit News and Historical Society of Michigan, 1991, p.26.
2. Material from Mary Marshall DAR Chapter publications.
3. Elizabeth L. Glynn, from Marshall Statesman 1854 obituary, Marshall Public Library, January 5, 1993.

Special thanks to John Collins, Marshall; Mary Marshall DAR Chapter, Mrs. John R. Atley, Marshall, September 1992.

MARY KIDDER BARRY   1842 through 1846

1. Sue I. Silliman, *St. Joseph in Homespun,* Three Rivers Publishing Co., 1931, p.168.
2. Claudius B. Grant, *Governors of the Territory and State of Michigan,* Edited by George N. Fuller, Bulletin No. 16, Michigan Historical Commission, Lansing, 1928.
3. Silliman, Ibid. p.168.
4. Silliman, Ibid. p.168.
5. H. H. Riley, *Pioneer Society of the State of Michigan,* Vol. XI, second edition, 1908, p.233.
6. Dr. Marvin Vercler, Constantine, as told to the author, May 16, 1992.
7. Silliman, Ibid. p.169.

Special thanks to Dr. Marvin Vercler, Governor Barry Historical Society president, January 1993.

LUCRETIA LAWRENCE FELCH   1846 into 1847

1. *The Monroe Evening News,* July 31, 1946.
2. Claudius B. Grant, *Governors of the Territory and State of Michigan,* Edited by George N. Fuller, Bulletin No. 16, Michigan Historical Commission, Lansing, 1928.
3. Felch Papers, Michigan Historical Collections, Bentley Historical Library, University of Michigan.
4. *Michigan Manual,* Michigan Department of Management and Budget, 1979-80, pp.88, 109, 110.
5. Felch Papers, Ibid.
6. *Portrait and Biographical Album of Jackson County Michigan,* Chapman Brothers, Chicago, Illinois, 1890.
7. Felch Papers, Ibid.
8. Felch Papers, Ibid.
9. *Michigan Manual,* Ibid., pps.105, 122 and 162.

Special thanks to Kenneth P. Scheffel, Bentley Historical Library, University of Michigan.

ELIZABETH HUBBARD GREENLY   1847

1. W. A. Whitney, *History and Biographical Album of Lenawee County*, W. Stearns and Company, 1879, Vol.1, p.101.
2. Ibid.
3. Bowen, *Gravestone Records of Lenawee County*, Vol. 1.
4. Whitney, Ibid.

Special thanks to Doris Frazier, Adrian, November 1992; Jean Frazier, Lansing, 1977; Shirley Ehnis, Reference Librarian, Adrian Public Library, January 1993 and Suzanne Wayda-Slomski, Adrian Public Library, April 14, 1993.

ALMIRA CADWELL RANSOM   1848 and 1849

1. *Portrait and Biographical Record of Kalamazoo, Allegan and Van Buren Counties, Michigan*, Chapman Brothers, Chicago, Illinois, 1892, p.797.
2. Joanne E. Dorgan, Kalamazoo, November 1992.
3. Wyllys Cadwell Ransom, *Ransom Family of America, Colchester Branch*, Richmond and Backus, Ann Arbor, 1903, p.98-99.
4. Ibid., p.140.
5. Pamphlet honoring Epaphroditus Ransom, with *Ransom Papers* in Local History section, Kalamazoo Public Library.
6. Wyllys Cadwell Ransom, Ibid., p.141.
7. Willis F. Dunbar, *Kalamazoo and How it Grew and Grew*, 1969.
8. Sandee Wallace, Interview with Carole M. Brinkmann, Herald Palladium, January 26, 1988.
9. *Kalamazoo Daily Telegraph*, March 19, 1877, p.4 and March 23, 1877, p.4, courtesy *Kalamazoo Gazette*, 1977.

Also see: *Governors of the Territory and State of Michigan*, Claudius B. Grant; *History of Kalamazoo County*, 1880, Everts and Abbott, Philadelphia, p. 117; Archives and Regional History Collections, Western Michigan University, 1992.

Special thanks to the late Alice Lammon, Kalamazoo, 1977; Kalamazoo Valley Genealogical Society, Comstock, 1992; Joanne E. Dorgan, Portage; Catherine A. Larson, Kalamazoo Public Library; Carole Brinkmann, St. Joseph; Jan Gibson Rickman, California; Margaret McComb, Midland; Rachel Gibson, Dowagiac; Arlys Derrick, *Herald Palladium*, St. Joseph and Peggy Guthaus, *Kalamazoo Gazette*.

MARY KIDDER BARRY   1850 and 1851
(See above)

SARAH SABIN McCLELLAND   1852 to March 8, 1853

1. Michigan Pioneer Collection, Michigan Historical Commission.
2. John McClelland Bulkley, *History of Monroe County Michigan*, The Lewis Publishing Co., 1913, p.256.
3. Ibid. p.257.
4. *Portrait and Biographical Album of Jackson County Michigan*, Chapman Brothers, Chicago, Illinois, May 1890.
5. Jean Frazier in statement to the author, 1977.
6. Donald M. D. Thurber, Grosse Pointe, MI, statement to the author, Sept. 24, 1992.

Special thanks to Matthew C. Switlik, Museum Director, Monroe County Historical Commission, January 1993.

ANNA MARILLA FERRAND S. PARSONS   1853 and 1854

1. *The Corunna Journal,* Corunna, Shiawassee County, Vol. XXI, No. 2, December 20, 1900, p.1.
2. Margaret Zdunic, Durand, citing 1850 U.S. Census, p.53A and Civil War enlistment papers of Charles Farrand Stewart.
3. Zdunic, Ibid., 1860 U.S. Census.
4. Jerry Roe, Vice President, Michigan Historical Commission, August 1992.
5. *Ancestors of Sarah Caroline Gulick,* by Joanne Nelson, Los Angeles, California, May 1992.
6. *Shiawassee County, MI, Marriage book B,* 1862-1867, cited by Mrs. Robert Couzynse, Owosso, MI, May 28, 1992.

Special thanks to Joanne Nelson, California, and Noreen Murphy, Owosso, August of 1992.

MARY WARDEN BINGHAM   1855 through 1858

1. *Biographies of Pioneers of Shiawassee and Clinton Counties,* 1880.
2. Letter from a daughter of Robert Warden, Constantine.
3. Letter, Ibid.
4. Mary Bingham, letter written from Green Oak, March 1841.
5. Mary Bingham, letter from Washington to "Lucinda" December 11, 1849.
6. *Fifty-two Years of Itinerate Life in the Michigan Conference of the Methodist Episcopal Church,* Rev. R. C. Crawford. 1856.
7. Edna Peach, South Lyon, in statement to author October 19, 1992.
8. Janet Rohrabacher, Howell, papers from "The Green Oak Historian," newsletter of the Green Oak Historical Society.

Special thanks to Janet Rohrabacher, Howell, October 1992; Rebecca Hewlett, Howell, 1977; Marge Driver and Edna Peach, Green Oak Historical Society, South Lyon, July 1992.

ANGEOLINA HASCALL WISNER   1859 and 1860

1. Alice Lethbridge, *Flint Journal,* July 1977.
2. Ruth G. Priestley, "The Moses Wisner Family 1815-1975," *Oakland Gazette,* November 1974, July 1977.
3. Claudius B. Grant, *Governors of the Territory and State of Michigan,* Bulletin No. 16, Michigan Historical Commission, Lansing, 1928.
4. *Portrait and Biographical Album of Jackson County,* Chapman Brothers, Chicago, Illinois, May 1890.
5. Priestley, Ibid.
6. Charles Martinez, Oakland County Pioneer and Historical Society, Pontiac, June 5, 1992.

Special thanks to Ruth G. Priestley, Waterford, September and November 1992.

SARAH HORTON FORD BLAIR   1861 through 1864

1. *Jackson Daily Citizen,* July 3, 1897.
2. *Jackson Daily Citizen,* August 7, 1884.
3. *The Historical Society of Michigan Newsletter,* March-April 1984.
4. Austin Blair Home, Part I, Nellie Blair Greene, *Jackson Tribune,* January 4, 1930. Provided by Kathryn E. Frank, Research Department, Jackson Public Library, July 1977.
5. Marion S. Grattan, *Jackson Citizen Patriot,* 1977.
6. Hilda Blackman, Montgomery, in a letter to the author, July 31, 1977.
7. Dick Frazier, *Lansing State Journal,* March 26, 1984, p B1.
8. Austin Blair Home, Ibid., Part II, provided by Betty Wier, Battle Creek, November 1992.

Also see: *Michigan Biographies*, Michigan Historical Commission, Volumes I and II, Lansing, 1924.

Special thanks to Helen Herman, the Sarah Treat Prudden Chapter, Daughters of the American Revoluton, Jackson; Helen King, Parish Historian, St. Mary's Catholic Church, Jackson; Mrs. John Wier, Battle Creek; Prof. Frederick D. Williams, Professor and Chairperson Emeritus, Department of History, Michigan State University, October, 1992; Donna Cannon, Jackson; Mount Evergreen Cemetery, Jackson, 1992.

MARY ANN SLOCUM CRAPO   1865 through 1868

1. Alice Lethridge, *Flint Journal*, 1977.
2. *Portrait and Biographical Album of Jackson County Michigan*, Chapman Brothers, Chicago, Illinois, May 1890.
3. Ibid.
4. Quotes courtesy Alice Lethridge, Ibid.
5. Lawrence R. Gustin, *Billy Durant, Creator of General Motors*, W. B. Eerdmans Publishing Co., Grand Rapids, 1973, p.27.
6. *Foundation for Living, The Story of Charles Stewart Mott and Flint*, by Clarence H. Young and William A. Quinn, McGraw-Hill Book Company, 1963, p.26.
7. Gustin, Ibid., p 31.

Also see: *Crapo papers*, Michigan Historical Collections, University of Michigan.

SIBYL LAMBARD BALDWIN   1869 through 1872

1. Chancey P. Miller, Elmwood Cemetery, Detroit, February 3, 1993.
2. Ibid.
3. *Dictionary of American Biography*, p. 534-35.
4. W. Hawkins Ferry, *The Buildings of Detroit*, Wayne State University Press, 1968, p.82.
5. *Detroit News*, April 27, 1922
6. *Los Angeles Times*, Courtesy Burton Historical Collection
7. *Detroit Free Press*, May 6, 1922

Special thanks to Christine Lahy, Birmingham; Noel VanGorden, Chief, Burton Historical Collection; Patience Nauta, Registrar, Historic Fort Wayne.

FRANCES NEWBERRY BAGLEY   1873 through 1876

1. *Michigan Manual*, 1873.
2. Claudius B. Grant, *Governors of the Territory and State of Michigan*, Edited by George N. Fuller, Bulletin No. 16, Michigan Historical Commission, Lansing, 1928.
3. Jean Frazier, Lansing, 1977.
4. *Portrait and Bibilographical Album of Jackson County Michigan*, Chapman Brothers, Chicago, Illinois, May 1890.

ELIZABETH MUSGRAVE CROSWELL   1877 through 1880

1. *Michigan Manual*, 1877.
2. *Adrian Woman's Club, Ninetieth Anniversary*, May 20, 1973, p.8.
3. Ibid.
4. *National Register of Historic Places*, U.S. National Park Service records.

Special thanks to: Doris A. Frazier, Adrian, July 1977 and Lucy Wolcott Barnum Chapter DAR, Adrian; Charles Lindquist, Lenawee County Historical Society, Inc., 1992.

LUCY PECK JEROME   1881 and 1882
1. *Michigan Manual*, 1979-80, Michigan Department of Budget and Management, p.88.
2. *Jerome Genealogy*, compiled by Elizabeth Jerome Brigati, provided by David and Kathlien Jerome, Northville, 1992.
3. *Minutes of the Saginaw Reading Club History*, 1885. Public Libraries of Saginaw, 1977.
4. *Genealogy*, Ibid., pg.14.
5. *Genealogy*, Ibid., pg.23.
6. James Cooke Mills, *History of Saginaw County Michigan*, Volume 1, page 331.
Special thanks to Kathlien Jerome, Northville, and Sandy L. Schwan, Registrar, Historical Society of Saginaw County.

HARRIET MILES BEGOLE   1883 and 1884
1. Alice Lethridge, *Flint Journal*, 1977.
2. *Portrait and Biographical Album of Jackson County Michigan*, Chapman Brothers, Chicago, Illinois, May 1890.

ANNETTE HENRY ALGER   1885 and 1886
1. *Portrait and Biographical Album of Jackson County Michigan*, Chapman Brothers, Chicago, Illinois, May 1890.
2. Rodney Bell, *Michigan History*, Vol. 64, January/February 1980, p.36.
3. Claudius B. Grant, *Governors of the Territory and State of Michigan*, Bulletin No. 16, Michigan Historical Commission, Lansing, 1928.
4. Grand Rapids Public Library, Local History Collection, December 28, 1992.
Other sources: Michigan State Library, 1977; Chancey P. Miller, Elmwood Cemetery, February 3, 1993 and Suzy Berscheack, Grosse Pointe War Memorial, March 24, 1993.

MARY BROWN THOMPSON LUCE   1887 through 1890
1. *Coldwater Daily Reporter*, January 19, 1920, p.1.
2. Viola A. Hawley, *Coldwater Daily Reporter*, 1977.
3. *Coldwater Daily Reporter*, Ibid.
4. Helen Luce, Coldwater, February 15, 1979, correspondence with author.
5. *Mackinac Island, The Story of the Straits Country*, by Robert E. Benjamin, p.58 and 63.
6. *Coldwater Daily Reporter*, Ibid., p.2.
Other sources: George Fuller, Ed., *Governors of the Territory and the State of Michigan*, Bulletin No. 16, Michigan Historical Commission, Lansing, 1928, pp.137-140; Carol Ankney, Burr Oak, January 1993.
Special thanks to Jeanne Moeller, Volunteer, Holbrook Heritage Room, Branch District Library, Coldwater, February 10, 1993.

ELIZABETH GALLOWAY WINANS   1891 and 1892
1. Claudius B. Grant, *Governors of the Territory and State of Michigan*, Michigan Historical Commission, Lansing, 1928.
2. *Livingston County Republican-Press*, July 1, 1936.
3. Ibid.
4. Rebecca Hewlett, Howell, 1977.
5. *Livingston County Republican-Press*, Ibid.

6. *Biographies of Pioneers of Shiawassee and Clinton Counties,* 1880, p.182.
7. Mrs. Ferdinand (Minnie M.) Cox in letter to the author, August 27, 1977 and statements to the author, November 1, 1977.
8. *Brighton Argus,* February 3, 1926 issue. Courtesy Green Oak Historical Society.
Special thanks to George Hull, Hamburg, July 8, 1992; Bonnie Van Wagnen, Jackson; Mrs. Janet Rohrabacher, Howell, October 1992; Philip Livingston Chapter DAR., Howell, 1992; Milton E. Charboneau, Curator, Howell Carnegie Library and Duane L. Zemper, photographer, Howell Library.

LUCRETIA WINSHIP RICH   1893 through 1896

1. Sam Painter, Davison, information to the author, July 1977.
2. Painter, Ibid.
3. Jean Frazier, *History of Sparrow Hospital,* Oct. 31, 1992
4. Claudius B. Grant, *Governors of the Territory and State of Michigan,* Michigan Historical Commission, Lansing, 1928.
5. George Weeks, *Stewards of the State: The Governors of Michigan,* The Detroit News and the Historical Society of Michigan, 1991, p.66.
6. Painter, statement to the author October 18, 1992.
Special thanks to the late Charles D. Braidwood, Archdeacon of Michigan, Lapeer, July 28, 1977.

FRANCES GILBERT PINGREE   1987 through 1900

1. *Michigan Manual,* 1897, Michigan Department of Management and Budget.
2. Detroit Historical Museum, records from Hazel (Pingree) Mills.
3. W. Hawkins Ferry, *The Buildings of Detroit,* Wayne State University Press, 1968, p.81.
4. Jean Frazier, Lansing, 1977
5. Melvin G. Holli, *Reform in Detroit; Hazen S. Pingree and Urban Politics,* Oxford University Press, 1969, p.215.
6. *Historical Markers and Memorials in Michigan,* Michigan History Magazine, Spring, 1931, p.1931.
Special thanks to Mrs. Gilbert (Katharine) Pingree, Grosse Pointe; C. Hazen Pingree, Fort Wayne, Indiana, February 1993; Patience Nauta, Registrar, Historic Fort Wayne, February 1993.

ALLASEBA PHELPS BLISS   1901 through 1904

1. Saginaw Public Library, clipping from *Saginaw News,* July 28, 1918.
2. *Saginaw News,* November 5, 1915, Courtesy Lorri Lea, Saginaw News Library Staff, August 1992.
3. *Saginaw News,* September 21, 1951.
4. *History of Saginaw County, Michigan,* James Cooke Mills, Seeman and Peters, Saginaw 1918, Vol 2, p.25.
5. *Saginaw News,* July 28, 1918.
6. *Saginaw News,* July 28, 1918.
Special thanks to the Historical Society of Saginaw County, Sandy L. Schwan, Registrar, May 1992; Anna Mae Thompson, Public Libraries of Saginaw, October 1977; Joan Ethridge, Public Libraries of Saginaw, May 1992.

MARTHA DAVIS WARNER   1905 through 1910

1. Edessa Slocum in a telephone interview with the author, 1977.

2. Jean M. Fox, "I Went to the People" *Fred M. Warner: Progressive Governor,* Farmington Hills Historical Commission, 1988, pp.104, 116, 188, 260, 350.

3. Jean M. Fox, Ibid.

Special thanks to Jean M. Fox and Charles R. Carvell, Farmington Historical Museum, June 3, 1992.

LILLIAN JONES OSBORN   1911 and 1912

1. Robert M. Warner, *Chase Salmon Osborn: 1860-1849,* University of Michigan, Ann Arbor, 1960.

2. Warner, Ibid.

3. Ann Osborn Pratt, telephone interview with author, August 9, 1977. Sault Ste. Marie.

4. Ann Osborn Pratt, correspondence with author, September 9, 1992.

5. Warner, Ibid.

6. Ann Osborn Pratt, Ibid.

Other sources: *Biographical Encyclopedia of America,* 1940, p.700-701; *Michigan Pioneers, The First One Hundred Years of Statehood,* J. L. Hudson Co., Detroit, 1937, p.130-133; *An Accolade for Chase S. Osborn,* published by the City of Sault Ste. Marie, in honor of his 80th Birthday, 1940.

Special thanks to Ann Osborn (Mrs. Stanley) Pratt.

HELEN GILLESPIE FERRIS   1913 through 1916

1. Woodbridge Nathan Ferris, *In Memory of Mrs. Helen Gillespie Ferris,* 1917. Ferris Papers, Historical Collections, Bentley Historical Library, University of Michigan.

2. Claudius B. Grant, *Governors of the Territory and the State of Michigan,* Michigan Historical Commission, Lansing, 1928.

3. Ferris Papers, Tribute by Lena Severance, p.13.

4. Grant, Ibid., p.175.

5. Ferris, Ibid., p.7.

6. Ibid., p.9.

Special thanks to R. Lawrence Martin, Coordinator, Archives, Ferris State University.

MARY MOORE SLEEPER   1917 through 1920

1. *Michigan Manual,* 1917.

2. Ivabel Spaulding, Recording Secretary of the Bad Axe Chapter of the Huron Historical Society. Sources: The Reverend Fr. James Sorrensen (Church Records), Miss Nora Dowde, Mrs. Henry Krueger and Mrs. Paul Soini.

3. Dr. Clark Herrington, (Sept. 1992) Mrs. Sleeper's Diaries.

4. George Weeks, *Stewards of the State: The Governors of Michigan,* The Detroit News and the Historical Society of Michigan, 1991, p.82.

6. Jerry Roe, Vice President, Michigan Historical Commission, August 1992

Special thanks to Dr. Clark Herrington, Bad Axe, for photograph and diaries, November 1992.

Governor Alexander Groesbeck   1921 through 1926

No hostess, no known wife.

HELEN KELLY GREEN   1927 through 1930

1. *Who's Who in Michigan,* 1936 edition, Munising.

2. *Michigan Manual,* 1929, pg 663.
3. Harry Boyes, Ionia, 1977 interview with author.
4. Helen N. Tyrrell, telephone interview with author, January 17, 1993.
5. Boyes, Ibid.
6. Tyrrell, Ibid.
7. Boyes, Ibid.
Special thanks to Helen N. Tyrrell, Sacramento, California, August 1992 and January 17, 1993; Ralph Bartelt, Ionia County Historical Society.

CLARA HANTEL BRUCKER   1931 and 1932
1. Patricia Chargot, *Detroit Free Press,* March 26, 1980, pg 18B.
2. Clara Brucker, telephone interviews and correspondence with the author, August, September and December 1977
3. Chargot, Ibid.
4. Patricia Wiggins, UPI, March 27, 1959.
5. Clara Brucker, Ibid.
6. Eleanor Breitmeyer, *Detroit News,* April 3, 1978.
7. Patricia Chargot, ibid.
Special thanks to Mrs. Wilber Brucker, Jr., Grosse Pte. Farms, May 1992.

MARY JOSEPHINE WHITE COMSTOCK   1933 and 1934
1. George Weeks, *Stewards of the State: The Governors of Michigan,* The Detroit News and the Historical Society of Michigan, 1991, p.92.
2. Maryanne Comstock, (Mrs. William Comstock III) in correspondence August 8, 1977 and telephone conversations, August 9, 1977 and November 9, 1977.
3. *Michigan Manual,* 1933.

QUEENA WARNER FITZGERALD   1935 AND 1936, 1939
1. Justice John W. Fitzgerald, telephone interview, July 20, 1977.
2. George Weeks, *"Stewards of the State: The Governors of Michigan,"* The Detroit News and the Historical Society of Michigan, 1991, p.96.
3. Ibid., p. 94.
4. Dick Frazier, *State Journal,* Jan. 27, 1985, pg B1.
5. Lorabeth Fitzgerald, May 8, 1977, and September 1992, telephone interview and correspondence with the author.

MARGUERITE MURPHY TEAHAN (Sister)   1937 AND 1938
1. Sidney Fine, *Frank Murphy: A Michigan Life,* Historical Society of Michigan, 1985, p.10-11.
2. Denise Bancroft, Lansing, August 2, 1977 and August 1992. Correspondence and conversation with the author.
3. Bancroft, Ibid., August 30, 1992.
4. Fine, Ibid., p.14.
5. Jerry Roe, August 1992, conversation with the author.
6. Bancroft, Ibid., August 30, 1992.
7. Fine, Ibid., p.1.

ZORA COOLEY DICKINSON   1939 and 1940

1. *Governor Luren D. Dickinson: Autobiography*, p.2.
2. Ibid., p.3.
3. Mrs. Frank Dickinson, Diamondale, August 4, 1977, statement to the author.
4. Pete Edick, Charlotte, letter to the author, August 1977.
5. William Kulsea, *The Governors: 50 Years Covering the Statehouse*, Michigan Business, December 1986, p.26.

HELEN JOSEPHINE JOSSMAN VAN WAGONER   1941 and 1942

1. Helen Van Wagoner, telephone interview with author, July 25, 1977.
2. Walter Wikol, Birmingham, statement to author, October 27, 1992.
3. Walter Wikol, Ibid.
4. *Detroit News*, April 24, 1986
5. *Jackson Citizen Patriot*, June 13, 1986, p.A9.
Also see: *Michigan Manual*, 1941; *Lansing State Journal*, Oct. 10, 1948 and April 1, 1951.
Special thanks to Walter Wikol, November 1992 and January 1993.

ANNE O'BRIEN KELLY   1943 through 1946

1. Mary Kelly James, Saginaw, Correspondence and conversation with author 1977; May and October 1992.
2. Ibid.
3. George Weeks, *Stewards of the State: The Governors of Michigan*, The Detroit News and the Historical Society of Michigan, 1991, Revised Second Edition, p.106.
4. *Michigan Manual*, 1939, p.586.

MAE PIERSON SIGLER   1947 and 1948

1. Kendrick Kimball, *Detroit News Pictorial*, January 19, 1947, p.12-13.
2. Madalon Gossett, McAlester, Oklahoma, conversation with the author, 1977
3. Esther Walton, from her column, *From Time to Time*.
4. Kendrick Kimball, Ibid.
5. Virginia Baird, information to the author, 1992.
6. Charles H. Churchill, *Michigan History*, Vol.1, No. 1, pp.1-3.
7. Baird, Ibid.
8. Beverly Ciciliano, Las Vegas, conversation with the author, January 16, 1993.
9. *Lansing State Journal*, October 23, 1963.
Special thanks to Virginia Baird, East Lansing; Virginia Hutcheson, East Lansing; Beverly Ciciliano, Las Vegas, Nevada; Maureen Ketchum, Hastings.

NANCY QUIRK WILLIAMS   1949 through 1960

1. George Weeks, *Stewards of the State: The Governors of Michigan*, The Detroit News and the Historical Society of Michigan, 1991, p.101.
2. Nancy Williams, conversation with the author, July 20, 1977.
3. *Lansing State Journal*, May 24, 1955.
4. Virginia Redfern, *Lansing State Journal*, May 27, 1979, p.C 1.
5. Nancy Williams Gram, conversation with the author, November 7, 1992.

ALICE NIELSEN SWAINSON   1961 and 1962

1. *Shipherd's Record of Olivet College*, Spring 1988, Volume III, No.2, p.1.

2. Alice Swainson, conversations with the author, June 1977 and November 14, 1992.

3. John Swainson, conversation with the author, November 10, 1992.

4. George Weeks, *Stewards of the State: the Governors of Michigan,* The Detroit News and the Historical Society of Michigan, 1991, p.119.

5. Ibid., p.119

6. *Shipherd's Record of Olivet College,* Ibid., p.1.

LENORE LaFOUNT ROMNEY   1963 into 1969

1. Lenore Romney in an interview with the author, March 1967.

Interviews and correspondence with the author from 1967 through 1992, are sources for all the quotes.

Special thanks to Governor George Romney.

HELEN WALLBANK MILLIKEN   1969 through 1982

1. Helen Milliken in an interview with the author, June 1977.

Interviews and correspondence with the author from 1977 through 1992, are sources for all quotes unless so noted.

2. Dan Angel, *William Milliken: A Touch of Steel,* Public Affairs Press, 1970, p.33

3. Joyce Braithwaite and George Weeks, *The Milliken Years: A Pictorial Reflection,* The Traverse City Record-Eagle and Village Press, Inc., 1988, p.27.

4. Malcolm Johnson, *Associated Press,* October 20, 1982.

PAULA PARKER BLANCHARD   1983 through 1986

1. Interview with the author October 4, 1983.

2. Correspondence with the author, July 20, l992.

JANET EIFERT FOX BLANCHARD   1989 through 1990

1. Telephone interview with Mrs. Howard Eifert, Mason, June 1992.

2. Correspondence with the author, June 19, 1992.

3. Charlie Cain, *Detroit News,* July 23, 1992.

MICHELLE DeMUNBRUN ENGLER   1991-

1. Interview with the author, June 6, 1991.

Interview and correspondence with author are sources for all quotes.

MICHIGAN WOMEN LIEUTENANT GOVERNORS

MATILDA R. DODGE WILSON   November 1940 to January 1940

1. Marion Marzolf and Marianne Ritchie, *Matilda R. Wilson, Mistress of Meadow Brook Hall,* Meadow Brook Hall publication, p.17.

2. Ibid. Marzolf and Ritchie, pp.3 and 4.

3. *Detroit News,* November 19, 1940.

4. Jean Maddern Pitrone and Joan Potter Elwart, *The Dodges—the Auto Family Fortune and Misfortune,* Icarus Press, Inc., South Bend, Indiana, 1981.

Special thanks to Marylin Brooks and Corenna Aldrich, Meadow Brook Hall, December 7, 1992.

MARTHA W. GRIFFITHS   1983 through 1990

1. Chris Christoff, *Going Down Swinging,* AARP Bulletin, October 1990, p.20.
2. William Ballenger III, *Jackson Citizen Patriot,* August 26, 1990, p.1.
3. Fran Harris, *Focus: Michigan Women 1701-1977,* Michigan State Coordinating Committee of the National Commission on the Observance of Women's Year, 1977, p.97.
4. Ibid. Christoff, p.20.
5. Ibid. Christoff, p.20.
6. Peter Luke, *Jackson Citizen Patriot,* May 10, 1990, p.1.
7. George Weeks, *Stewards of the State: The Governors of Michigan,* The Detroit News and the Historical Society of Michigan, 1991, p.153.

Special thanks to Pam Gawronski, Librarian, Lansing State Journal, November 1992.

CONNIE B. BINSFELD   1991-

1. Gary Mills, *Lansing State Journal,* January 27, 1992, p.1B.
2. Kathy Barks Hoffman, *Lansing State Journal,* November 29, 1990, p.2A.
3. Interviews with the author, May 1977 and correspondence December 1992. All information, unless otherwise noted, from Lt. Gov. Connie Binsfeld.

GOVERNOR'S FAMILY RESIDENCES

1. Annie Hogoboom, Residences Manager, January 8, 1993.
2. Joan Richardson, *Detroit Free Press Magazine,* June 24, 1990, p.18.
3. Jerry Moskal, *Lansing State Journal,* June 28, 1981, p.2.
4. *The Governor's Summer Residence,* Mackinac Island State park Commission, 1977.
5. George Weeks, *Stewards of the State: The Governors of Michigan,* The Detroit News and the Historical Society of Michigan, 1991, p.178.
6. Paula Blanchard, Interview with the author, October 4, 1983.
7. Michelle Engler, Interview with the author, June 6, 1991.

❖ Governors ❖
of the State of Michigan

Governor	Party Affiliation	Years in Office
John M. Engler	Republican	1991-
James J. Blanchard	Democrat	1983-1990
William G. Milliken	Republican	1969-1982
George W. Romney	Republican	1963-1969
John B. Swainson	Democrat	1961-1962
G. Mennen Williams	Democrat	1949-1960
Kim Sigler	Republican	1947-1948
Harry F. Kelly	Republican	1943-1946
Murray D. Van Wagoner	Democrat	1941-1942
Luren D. Dickinson	Republican	1939-1940
Frank D. Fitzgerald	Republican	1939
Frank Murphy	Democrat	1937-1938
Frank D. Fitzgerald	Republican	1935-1936
William A. Comstock	Democrat	1933-1934
Wilber M. Brucker	Republican	1931-1932
Fred W. Green	Republican	1927-1930
Alexander J. Groesbeck	Republican	1921-1926
Albert E. Sleeper	Republican	1917-1920
Woodbridge N. Ferris	Democrat	1913-1916
Chase S. Osborn	Republican	1911-1912
Fred M. Warner	Republican	1905-1910
Aaron T. Bliss	Republican	1901-1904

Hazen S. Pingree	Republican	1897-1900
John T. Rich	Republican	1893-1896
Edwin B. Winans	Democrat	1891-1892
Cyrus G. Luce	Republican	1887-1890
Russell A. Alger	Republican	1885-1886
Josiah W. Begole	Fusion	1883-1884
David H. Jerome	Republican	1881-1882
Charles M. Croswell	Republican	1877-1880
John J. Bagley	Republican	1873-1876
Henry P. Baldwin	Republican	1869-1872
Henry H. Crapo	Republican	1865-1868
Austin Blair	Republican	1861-1864
Moses Wisner	Republican	1859-1860
Kinsley S. Bingham	Republican	1855-1858
Andrew Parsons	Democrat	1853-1854
Robert McClelland	Democrat	1852-1853
John S. Barry	Democrat	1850-1851
Epaphroditus Ransom	Democrat	1848-1849
William L. Greenly	Democrat	1847
Alpheus Felch	Democrat	1846-1847
John S. Barry	Democrat	1842-1845
James W. Gordon	Whig	1841
William Woodbridge	Whig	1840-1841
Stevens T. Mason	Democrat	1835-1839